"LET ME BE WEAK"
What People in Pain Wish They Could Tell You

BRITTANY BARBERA

Let Me Be Weak

Cover design: Publish My Book Today
Formatting: Publish My Book Today
Author Photo: Susie Aboulhosn

DEDICATION

To those who have been courageous enough to
trust me with their pain:

I love you all.

And to everyone who aspires to be like them:

You are my people.

FREE DIGITAL DOWNLOAD

READ THIS FIRST

Just to say thanks for purchasing my book, I would like to give you one of my songs, "Yet I Will Praise," for FREE!

In addition to the free music, you will be the first to know when my new single,
"Let Me Be Weak," is available for purchase,
and have access to behind the scenes videos of the recording process.

Grab your FREE DIGITAL DOWNLOAD today:

(**http://brittanybarbera.com/letmebeweakfreemusicdownload**)

TABLE OF CONTENTS

ACKNOWLEDGMENTS vii

DISCLAIMER ix

INTRODUCTION...xi

1. "I KNOW I SEEM ALRIGHT…" 1

2. "IT'S BEEN A LONG AND LONELY ROAD" 17

3. "I NEED A SAFE PLACE TO LAND" 35

4. "WOULD YOU BE KIND AND HOLD OUT YOUR HAND?" 47

5. "YOU DON'T HAVE TO FIND THE WORDS TO SAY" ... 57

6. "WE DON'T ALWAYS KNOW IF WE'RE GOING TO BE OKAY" 69

7. "DON'T TRY TO FIX ME; I DON'T NEED YOUR CRITIQUE" 81

8. "JUST BE STRONG" 93

9. "LET ME BE WEAK"... 101

10. "WHEN THERE'S NOTHING LEFT TO DO, YOU'LL HAVE TO PRAY ME THROUGH"...................................... 111

11. "GIVE ME TIME; I NEED TO HEAL"............................... 119

"LET ME BE WEAK".

12. "I DON'T WANT TO HIDE THE WAY I FEEL".............125

EPILOGUE... 133

ABOUT THE AUTHOR... 135

LET ME BE WEAK... 137

YET I WILL PRAISE 138

BE STILL MY SOUL... 139

GOD MOVES IN A MYSTERIOUS WAY 140

NOTES... 143

ACKNOWLEDGMENTS

To my family and friends, whose love, support, and prayers have carried me thus far—thank you. Without all of you, I would not be the person I am today, and I certainly wouldn't have nearly as many stories to tell.

Specifically, to my mom, Debra Barbera—who has been telling me to write this book for years; I finally listened. Thank you for teaching me what it looks like to care for others and remain steadfast to the truth even when the journey is hard.

To Chandler Bolt, Sean Sumner, and the phenomenal team at Self-Publishing School—thank you for convincing me to write this book and inspiring me throughout the process. Your enthusiasm is contagious and your practical advice has helped me turn my dream into a reality.

To my friend, Erin Pearson—thank you for listening to my crazy ideas and helping me work through a few meltdowns. I'm grateful for your support and I'm even more grateful that you decided to write a book of your own, so we could write them together! Thank you for being my faithful "writing date," day after day, and for being patient with me all those times I accidentally kicked your broken leg.

To my friend and editor, Lisa Detweiler Miller—I've loved collaborating with you for the past decade, and I've loved your friendship more. If I were Tina Fey, you'd definitely be my Amy Poehler. Thank you for sacrificing what little sleep you get in order to help this book reach its potential; your insights have made it exponentially better.

To my friend, Jane Lindemuth—your faith and perseverance in times of adversity are inspirational. You've shown me what it looks like to model many of the principles in this book, and that is a true gift.

To the SPS Mastermind Community and my incredible Launch Team—thank you for your encouragement, suggestions, generosity, and humor. You all have made this process much more enjoyable!

DISCLAIMER

My fear in writing this book is that people will see it as an excuse to let their emotions dominate their lives and guide their behaviors. It is disheartening to think that they might interpret the insight and stories in this book as permission to stay in their pain and refuse to work through their issues.

However, that is not what this book is about.

It is not about teaching people to be become better enablers by perpetuating a cycle of helplessness. It is not about embracing a victim mentality or prolonging the healing process.

Instead, it is written on behalf of those who, during seasons of heartache and suffering, are struggling to find their way. And more specifically, it is for the people in their lives who care deeply and want to help, but lack the understanding to know what to do.

INTRODUCTION

To be human is to be vulnerable. Even the most powerful among us are susceptible to having an off day, or week, or year. Regardless of how well put together we may look on the outside, the unavoidable truth is this: everyone feels overwhelmed sometimes. Though we are often seduced by the glamour of invincibility, life happens to us all—people or dreams die and relationships end. Jobs we depend on for financial stability dissolve in the wake of economic uncertainty. Accidents and illness prey upon the loveliest of people, and catch us off guard. All manner of unexpected traumas threaten to interrupt our plans, turn our world upside down, and expose the cracks in our armor.

However, we live in a culture where we are encouraged to be self-sufficient, where the powerful are celebrated and even idolized. According to Peggy Yuhas Byers, a communication researcher who examines the ways in which organizations convey their commonly held beliefs, "Stories are thought to be a particularly effective means of transmitting culture because as stories are retold over time, the themes and values they express become real" to its members.[1] As such, when our media bombards us with unrealistic images of what our lives should look like, and we, in turn, adopt those messages as our own, we risk glorifying a reality that does not actually exist. In communities across America, on both the macro and micro levels, we esteem self-made men and women and seek to emulate their success. While there is nothing wrong with admiring the accomplishments and influence of these inspiring individuals, when we do not also talk about their obstacles and insecurities, we tell an incomplete story. As a result, we suffer the silent shame of inferiority when our lives don't measure up, because we have mistakenly believed a lie.

When our media bombards us with unrealistic images of what our lives should look like, and we, in turn, adopt those messages as our own, we risk glorifying a reality that does not actually exist.

When crisis hits, our deep seated ideology of independence spills over into the way we care for people in pain. We struggle to allow room for grief and are tempted to resist the necessary work of healing because it is a messy and uncomfortable process. Our desire to help the people we love navigate their way during a season of loss, coupled with our lack of understanding about how to actually implement that help, leaves us feeling frustrated and helpless.

This book is about what to do when we are confronted with painful situations that simultaneously demand a response and evoke internal resistance. It's about shedding light on the many struggles people face during seasons of loss and learning how we can help them through it. It's about honoring those courageous enough to admit their limitations and ask for what they need. It's giving ourselves permission to feel our feelings, even when they make us uncomfortable. It's about increasing our capacity for compassion towards ourselves and others and learning to listen without an agenda. It's being willing to wait and hope even when the answers don't come. It's having faith that the whole world won't fall apart, even if someone we love does.

In the sacred moments of heartbreak and hope, we will all need to be reminded that we are not alone and that our weaknesses don't define us or make us unworthy of love.

Mostly, however, this book is about us—all of us. Eventually, every one of us will take a turn on each side; we will know alternately what it is to be the helper and what it is to be the one in need of help. In the sacred moments of heartbreak and hope, we will all need to be reminded that we are not alone and that our weaknesses don't define us or make us unworthy of love.

I'm not a counselor by trade, but what I lack in formal training I make up for in empathy and hours upon hours of revealing conversations. I've heard countless stories and witnessed first-hand the horrible things people say to each other in times of emotional distress or crisis, all in the name of being helpful. Too often, we allow our own discomfort to dictate our behaviors, which, ultimately, denies people the time they need to process their emotions and heal, and that bothers me.

I'm an extreme feeler—the highs, lows, and everything in between—it matters to me. Until a few years ago, I saw this part of myself as a serious liability, as though sensitivity were something I needed to overcome, not embrace. In fact, when I heard about the Strengths Finders book and accompanying personal assessment, I was all too eager to take the test and discover my top strengths.[2] When I learned "empathy" was at the top of my list, I thought it had to be a mistake. I was so disappointed because I wanted to excel at something *much cooler*. I'm not sure what I was expecting, but "congratulations, you're a total sap" definitely was not it. At the time, I was shocked and unappreciative because I failed to recognize the value of the gift that was given to me.

However, with the newfound wisdom of incredible researchers like Brené Brown, I started to change my perspective. I no longer apologize for having strong emotions because I am not sorry I have the ability to feel. Much to my surprise, I've also learned that empathy is incredibly useful. It's a relational superfood, the kale of the interpersonal world. Just like kale, however, we need to be convinced empathy is good for us or we might reject it outright.

I no longer apologize for having strong emotions because I am not sorry I have the ability to feel.

For a properly nourished soul, it's important to have a daily dose of empathy in our diet so we can reap the rewards of a healthier internal dialogue and deeper interpersonal relationships. Empathy is a fundamental aspect to every healthy relationship, because it is a connecting emotion. It seeks understanding, and without it, we will never be able to achieve the intimacy we desire in our relationships. In fact, Jamie George, a storyteller and pastor, suggests that "empathy is the ability to project oneself into someone else's narrative and see the world as they see it. If [we] have a connection problem, [we] have an empathy problem, which probably means [we] have a listening problem."[3]

It takes courage to look at our weakness and admit our insecurities. It requires even more courage to share the unedited version of our story with other people, especially when we don't know how it will be received. However, when we are willing to push past the fear and discomfort, when we are willing to listen and withhold judgment, we start to create an environment where it is safe to let our guard down. We start to become the kind of people others can trust with their pain, and we could all stand to have a few more people like that in our world.

Though we applaud the type of bravery a hero calls upon to save the day, it loses its appeal when, in humility, it looks more like someone admitting they are at the end of their rope. Regardless, both portray immense courage; they are members of the same family. They may be distinctly different in personality and form, but, in all the ways that matter, they are the same. Still, for many of us, it's a challenge to accept that as truth.

For a properly nourished soul, it's important to have a daily dose of empathy in our diet so we can reap the rewards of a healthier internal dialogue and deeper interpersonal relationships.

Unless we honestly believe the courage required to share our weakness is worth the loss of pride we feel when we admit our need, we will remain exactly as we are. We will continue to adhere to the cultural norms we've grown accustomed to, and we will forfeit countless opportunities to help or ask for help along the way. However, if we are willing to tell the truth, we will be better able to care for ourselves and others when we find ourselves in a sorrowful season of life. We will start to develop a healthier response to those who are mourning, one that is rooted in compassion and understanding. Instead of offering advice and trying to fix everything, we will gradually learn to shut our mouths and listen to what our brokenhearted friends need to tell us. If we're quiet long enough, they might even muster up the courage to utter the words they've been wanting to share all along. In the midst of their overwhelming pain and loss, maybe all they want to say is simply:

"Let me be weak."

1.

"I KNOW I SEEM ALRIGHT…"

People tell me things. Personal things. Embarrassing things. Weird things, for sure. In my circle of friends, I'm the one everyone calls in a crisis, and, over time, I started to wonder why. Maybe it's because I've been through my fair share of trauma and have come out on the other side arguably sane. Or maybe it's because my name begins with the letter "B" and it's the first one people see when they start scrolling through their contact list. Jury's still out.

Either way, I get a lot of these calls. In recent years, I've had a front row seat to the most devastating moments in my friends' lives, and I am grateful they have trusted me enough to invite me into their pain. Speechless and in shock, the majority of the time, I could only manage to listen. Fortunately for me, it turns out the simple act of listening to someone tell their story has a profound effect. It's amazing what people will tell us, if we just let them.

Somewhere along the line, however, listening stopped being about paying attention and seeking understanding and became that part of conversation when we're thinking of what we're going to say next to prove our point. We have a tendency to shift our focus from the person sharing and inadvertently make the interaction about us. By and large, we've become so preoccupied with how we feel about what is being said and whether or not we agree with it, that we often don't hear what is being said at all.

It's amazing what people will tell us, if we just let them.

Unfortunately, these habits have become so commonplace that they have permeated our culture and strongly influenced the way we communicate with one another, even in times of crisis. Instead of being fully present with people in pain and listening to their struggles, we are fixated on finding solutions and searching for rational explanations where none exist. When we cannot find a satisfying answer, we just pretend like we never had any questions. As a result, we subtly pressure people in pain to play along, so that we don't have to deal with the discomfort of the truth, and, in the process, we all become incredible secret keepers.

I'm a bit of a lone wolf in group discussions about sensitive subjects, but it's not because people can't relate to the things I say. I've often shared something publically only to be met with blank stares and silence. For the longest time, I couldn't figure it out. It was particularly baffling when some of people present for the discussion had previously shared a similar sentiment with me in private. Time and again, I would share how I felt, but few were willing to add to the conversation. I'd look around the room in vain and wonder if anyone else would speak up.

Crickets.

If the story ended there, I would have thought I was out of touch, or worse, crazy. However, that's usually when things would start to get interesting. Slowly but surely, people would secretly approach me afterwards. They'd stop me on the way out the door and tell me their stories. They'd say they were glad I spoke up because they identified with my feelings and experienced the same struggles. They'd send me emails, ask me questions, and thank me for sharing.

The same thing happened when I announced I was writing this book. Many people were immediately resistant to both the subject matter and the title. They wanted me to rename the book something more positive like, "Becoming Stronger." After all, weakness is not particularly appealing. For many, the idea of allowing people to experience pain and admit their weakness without simultaneously forcing them to make a plan about how to "get over it" is offensive.

Predictably, after the feigned disinterest, people started to reach out to me privately. Surprisingly, many of those who were interested in talking to me and learning more about the book were not the people I would have expected. I started wondering why people were willing to tell me their secrets and then pretend they felt the exact opposite in public. I asked a few probing questions and the responses came pouring in.

In conversation after conversation, everyone reiterated the same things. Either, they didn't have anyone to talk to, or, worse, they didn't want to talk to the people who insisted on talking to them. No one seemed to understand what they were going through, and though a few wanted to openly share their experience, they were terrified of being judged. They weren't willing to risk rejection because they desperately needed a sense of connection even if it lacked the depth they wanted. Everyone shared the same fears and almost everyone felt incredibly alone. They felt like they were the only ones who had ever felt the way they were feeling. As the depth of their pain threatened to consume them, many wondered if they would ever be happy again. Others wondered if they'd ever want to be happy again because, more than learning to flourish in their "new normal," what they really wanted was their old life back, but that was no longer an option.

Despite their internal pain, life kept on going. Their responsibilities didn't suddenly stop because they didn't have the energy to deal with them anymore. Many were the sole providers of their families. They had to force themselves to function when they wanted to stay in bed all day. Eventually, other people moved on and forgot what they never will. Life continued to force them into routines, and, day by day, they would trek on. To the outside world, it seemed as though they were doing alright, even though they were still in the throes of anguish, grief, and heartbreak. Surprisingly, even when people are in deep pain, they are very committed to making sure everyone else thinks they are fine.

Instead of being fully present with people in pain and listening to their struggles, we are fixated on finding solutions and searching for rational explanations where none exist.

Since neediness is not a desirable trait, the bereaved often fear they will become a burden to their friends and family. They may put undue pressure on themselves and try to overcompensate in an attempt to shield their loved ones from the pain they are experiencing. Scott Sauls says, "External bravado is often a cover-up for internal fear and insecurity."[1] Though they may be able to maintain a stiff upper lip, deep down, many are hiding the severity of their emotional distress. The temptation to appear more put together than is actually the case can be especially true for people who are very successful or are leaders within their communities. It's embarrassing, shameful even, to be unexpectedly shaken if you've been able to accomplish so much in other realms of life.

When the illusion of control is shattered, it leaves us with an overwhelming sense of vulnerability, which usually is the very feeling we're trying to avoid, by attempting to control everything. If I've learned anything at all, it's that fame, the amount of money in your bank account, or the number of awards you've received are all irrelevant when it comes to pain. Hurt is hurt and it doesn't care who you are or what you've accomplished. When people are hurting, they need emotional support, even those who consider their desire for help a "dirty little secret," those with the toughest exteriors, have a breaking point. Deep down, the ache is there, and they desperately hope to find someone who will "get it."

Everyone wants to be loved and accepted just as they are. Everyone. Maybe we don't need to feel loved by the masses, but, at the very least, we need to feel loved by the people closest to us. John Ortberg says, "[We] can only love and be loved to the extent that [we] know and are known by somebody."[2] Being known is the scary part. It requires us to be courageously vulnerable and tell the truth. It requires us to risk the rejection we so deeply fear.

We live in a culture that makes this kind of honesty difficult. We are so driven to impress, that we often think we are doing well as long as it appears that way externally. At the very least, we feel pressured to make sure our peers think we're okay. Though we are heavily influenced by mainstream culture, we are also heavily influenced by the various social groups to which we belong. Since we are members of many different communities, each with its own set of shared values and practices, the way each community responds to grief is likely to be different, and occasionally, counturcultural. For instance, in the Jewish community, there is a period of formal mourning, called "Shiva" that lasts for 7 days. In other communities, however, the grieving rituals are not as explicitly expressed and are communicated in an implicit manner. Ironically, even the places where we most desire to share the truth are sometimes the hardest places to actually be truthful. In the Christian community, a group I am a member of, we often struggle to fully embrace our painful experiences. It's easy to be confused and think we are doing all the right things simply because we want to be doing all the right things. However, when we offer up trite and insensitive opinions about why God allowed something bad to happen to someone, we shut down conversation and insult the grieving.

Hurt is hurt and it doesn't care who you are or what you've accomplished.

Instead of acknowledging the ugly emotions people experience in their suffering, we have a tendency to bypass them in favor of theological reasoning. When we refuse to ask them how they are feeling or recognize their emotions as legitimate, we encourage them to adhere to a façade rather than share their story unreservedly. Thus, we perpetuate a culture where it is nearly impossible to live authentically.

We are especially at risk for this type of behavior when we focus on the external. It is entirely possible for an unhealthy person to appear healthy and vice versa. Consider how grief might present itself in opposite ways, and varying degrees of health, in different individuals. On the outside, one individual might seem fairly put together, especially in lieu of their circumstances. They may not be overly emotional and may be able to manage their daily responsibilities at work, home and within the community. Externally, it would appear that person is coping with their loss quite well. Perhaps they are healthy and thriving against all odds. However, it is also possible that same individual is in an incredibly vulnerable place and resisting the work of healing. Instead of facing their grief head on, they could be delaying the inevitable because they cannot or do not want to fully accept their loss. Though they may appear to be the epitome of health, in actuality, they could be far from it. On the flip side, another bereaved person may look like a complete disaster as they faithfully walk the path of healing. Things often get worse before they get better, and someone who seems to be a complete mess, might simply be working through their pain. When an individual has been through a traumatic event, it is completely understandable and even healthy to feel its terrible sting. Though it's a necessary and appropriate reaction, it is not pretty.

My friend recently told me a story that demonstrates this paradox so clearly. She was on vacation in the mountains, sitting inside a yurt. I didn't know what that was, but she informed me it's like a tent, with a glass pane at the top, for the sun to shine in. As she sat there, she looked up and saw a hummingbird flying around the top of the yurt, near the glass. It was obvious that the bird was attracted to the sunlight shining in through the glass and wanted to go back outside. However, she understood what the bird could not: the only way to freedom would be to fly back down and out through the opening on the side of the tent.

In times of loss, many people behave like a hopeful but confused hummingbird. They crave relief from their heartache, not a full time job as an emotional storm chaser, because it's exhausting to scan for the potential threats lying dormant inside of themselves. Instead, it is enticing to believe the lie that they have already dealt with the full weight of their pain and are only a small step away from total healing. However, they cannot always see the barriers obstructing their way, or recognize the additional layers of grief brewing under the surface.

If our loved one is further away from healing than they suspect, pretending they are dealing with their loss better than they are is of no service to them. We can all lose our way and our perspective. However, we need to gently encourage those who are hurting to engage their hurt instead of running away from it. The hard truth is that, sometimes, the only way out is down. We have to be willing to sit with them in the mess and give them permission to process their emotions as they gradually move through their pain.

However, we can't ask people to go where we are unwilling to go ourselves. We have to be willing to go first because we cannot expect others to be vulnerable with us if we refuse to acknowledge our own vulnerabilities. We have to be willing to drop the act and tell the truth, so that the people we love will be willing to do the same. Yet, if we allow cultural expectations to rule our relationships, we will continue to wear our masks and hinder authenticity.

Pretending we have it all together and manipulating our image, robs us of a healthy self-esteem, and it keeps us from having the relationships we want.

Erving Goffman, who is widely regarded as one of the most influential sociologists of the last century, spent the majority of his career studying the mundane exchanges of everyday life. He popularized the use of dramaturgical analysis, a term he borrowed from the theatre and applied to sociology, and then used theatrical metaphor as a lens through which to examine the social interactions of an individual. In his most famous work, *The Presentation of Self in Everyday Life,* Goffman introduces us to the concept of "impression management," in which he suggests that people, like actors, have various motivations driving their interactions, and they alter the way they present themselves based on the way they want to be perceived.[3]

He identifies two distinct kinds of activity present in each interaction, which he refers to as "the impression given" and the "impression given off."[4] On the surface, this may seem to be an issue of semantics, but the differences in each concept are significant. The "impression given" is the more calculated, less genuine of the two. For example, if you are going on a first date and want to make a good impression, you might consciously alter the way you communicate in order to appear smart, funny, and successful. In other words, you are able to manage the impression you give by including certain cultural references in conversation, and maybe even changing your physical appearance and attire to make sure you look the part. As a result, those choices reinforce the message you want to send to your date and inform your date's opinion about who you are and how you operate in the world. It is a conscious effort and you behave according to a pre-planned persona, although not necessarily a sinister one.

Alternatively, the "impression given off" refers to the part of our interactions we cannot control and, as such, reveals our true attitudes and emotions through nonverbal clues and unintentional messages. It's certainly a rarity, if not a total impossibility, to ignore every impulse we have to influence the way other people think about us. However, the "impression given off" is our more genuine self, subtly sneaking out in our interactions without a targeted agenda. An example of this would be going to a party, meeting someone new and conversing with them. Since you are interested in the conversation and having fun, you smile and laugh frequently. Perhaps you even touch the person you're chatting with at some point, effortlessly building rapport. Upon leaving the party, your new friends remark to each other about your friendly and engaging personality and look forward to spending time with you in the future. This, at its core, is the essence of the "impression given off"; it is the way people perceive who you naturally are, without trying to manipulate their perspective.

Unfortunately, we live in a culture whose values align stronger with "the impression given" than with the sincerity of the "impression given off." We try to control the public's perception of us and secretly hope the image we present is so convincing that no one will notice any evidence to the contrary. However, this behavior causes all kinds of problems in our internal lives and interpersonal relationships, particularly when we are experiencing emotional pain. Over the years, I've seen this play out in a variety of ways, but it never leads anywhere good.

The disparity between an individual's public persona and the reality of their personal life is far too common in this day and age. As a musician, I've seen some drastic examples of this, in which some people are so consumed with their image that they sacrifice their integrity on the altar of fame and fortune. Privately, however, they have an ever-growing reputation, which may even directly contradict their professional platform. It's easy to think this kind of thing is only common among people in the public eye, but I can think of just as many examples from my time spent working in other industries. In fact, many people go to great lengths to impress their peers and pretend their way into financial ruin in order to protect a false image they created.

When we offer up trite and insensitive opinions about why God allowed something bad to happen someone, we shut down conversation an insult the grieving.

I don't even need to look for outside examples of this because I can think of times in my own life when I've done the same thing, and I know you can too. If you're having a hard time thinking of something, look no further than your social media platform of choice. I once heard someone say, "May your life be as awesome as you pretend it is on Facebook." It seems fitting because we have become masters at constructing semi-accurate realities in the cyber world.

So what do we do about this and why should we even care? The simple answer is this: pretending to have it all together and manipulating our image, robs us of a healthy self-esteem, and it keeps us from having not only the relationships we want but also the relationships we need. It makes us think we're not enough and everyone else is living a better life than we are; it breeds jealousy and envy.

Though Darren Whitehead warns us not to "compare what we know about [ourselves] with what [we] don't know about someone else," when we do not listen, we invite all kinds of irrational thoughts and snap judgments into our lives.[5] It gradually becomes normal to see others through the lens of competition and never actually see them. But just because it's the norm, does not mean it is healthy.

If we are saturated in a world where everyone else eats and drinks perfection and we find ourselves struggling, we are not going to volunteer that information. Instead, we will want to retreat inside and suppress our emotions. We will feel alone at a time when we most need community. I've experienced this to be especially true as it relates to how we process, understand, and interact with the people in our lives who are in emotional pain. We've become a culture intolerant of grief, loss, and sadness. Yet, in every corner of the world, people are grieving and experiencing loss and sadness, and no one knows what to do with them.

Our best intentions buckle under the weight of our discomfort, as the fear of what we cannot control bullies us into a corner and renders us paralyzed. Confusion and frustration only intensify, as we feel increasingly unqualified to help the suffering and are confronted with the unavoidable reality that someone we love desperately needs our help. Though we desire to ease the burden of hurt, we will unintentionally add to the pain, unless we find a way to sit in the discomfort and wrestle with the very things we want to run from. Fear tries to intimidate us into inaction, but each time we are willing to engage that which frightens us, we steal a little of its power and increase our capacity to comfort the brokenhearted in our midst.

2.

"IT'S BEEN A LONG AND LONELY ROAD"

Hiding our true feelings only leads us further away from the relationships we want because there are consequences to pretending. Unless we are willing to take off our masks and embrace the truth, even if we don't like what we find, we'll never have the depth of connection we desire. We may be able to fool ourselves into thinking our relationships are just fine, at least for a little while. Then, when crisis hits and someone is in pain, all of these latent issues are suddenly exposed and come to a head.

Few of us are able to support the people we love in their time of need, at least not in the way they need it. The cynic would argue that it's because most people simply don't care, but that is not my experience. I believe most people care more than we give them credit for, but caring falls short when they don't know what to do. When we don't know how to help, we feel helpless. As a result, our "help" doesn't actually feel like help to the person receiving it, and we struggle to give them what they need. We watch our loved one's fragile state continually decline, and it's horrifying.

We fear that if we say or do the wrong thing, it might be too much for our loved one to bear, and we don't want to be responsible for sending them over the edge. Since we don't know what to say or because we've tried really hard to help but couldn't, we gradually start to back away. It's tough work to stay engaged in an emotionally charged situation, particularly when there is no resolution in sight. We assume giving the bereaved their space is for the best because we don't want to make matters worse.

However, a person in pain does not see withdrawal as a sign of concern. They might not have the energy or ability to consider why you are not engaging them anymore because they are so consumed with their own pain. To them, it just looks like their friends don't care about them and don't understand the suffering they are experiencing. They feel disappointed and rejected, inflicting a wound that makes their already overwhelmed heart break a little more.

When people feel misunderstood, they also feel emotionally unsafe.

We've already discussed how hard it is for us to admit when we are struggling because there are so many fears tied up in that issue. Many people who are hurting keep silent, though, deep down, they don't want to keep their pain a secret. It takes a great deal of vulnerability to share our wounds because it makes us feel insecure and embarrassed. As friends and supporters, we need to cultivate a willingness to listen when we are afraid and uncomfortable. It is so important that we receive their words with grace and sensitivity when our friends and family are courageous enough to tell us the truth. It's a sacred moment when someone lets their guard down and lets us into their mess.

When we do not affirm them because of our own fears or lack of understanding about how to help, we send the wrong message. Failure to respond to their pain in an appropriate manner risks damage to the relational bond— the very outcome we have been trying to avoid. In his talk at Stanford University, lecturer Matt Abrahams says, "When [people] feel you are challenging [them], [they're] going to do the bare minimum to respond and protect [themselves]. If [they] see this as an opportunity to explain and expand, [they're] going to interact differently with you."[1]

In other words, when people feel misunderstood, they also feel emotionally unsafe. Their defense mechanisms creep into conversation because they want to protect themselves. The desire to guard their fragile heart often leads people to emotionally withdraw and retreat internally where they feel more secure. This tendency to remove themselves from their relationships is especially dangerous for those in pain because losing the connections where they previously felt safe, makes them even more vulnerable. It leaves them feeling isolated at a time when they most need the support of the people who love them. Many feel detached and disoriented and fear they will be left to cope with their grief alone.

While it is a nice sentiment to tell a grief-ridden friend to "let us know if we can do anything for them," it indirectly makes them responsible for our behavior, and lets us off the hook when they are too tired to think of anything.

Psychologist Guy Winch describes the type of mental and emotional pain lonely people experience through a personal story about when he was confronted with this anguish in himself. One year, on his birthday, he and his twin brother were living in different countries, but they planned to speak over the phone. As he anxiously awaited his brother's call, he grew increasingly upset. He spent the whole night inventing stories about why his brother never called, most of which assumed that his brother didn't care about him anymore and was too busy spending time with the new friends he made. The next morning, he discovered that, in his frantic pacing the night before, he had accidentally kicked the phone off the hook. When the two men eventually spoke, his brother didn't understand why he didn't just initiate the call himself, once he realized his brother hadn't called him first. It took years of psychological study to give him the insight he needed to finally identify "loneliness" as the answer to his brother's question.

Winch explains, "Loneliness creates a deep psychological wound. One that distorts our perceptions and scrambles our thinking. It makes us believe that those around us care much less than they actually do. It makes us really afraid to reach out because why set yourself up for rejection and heartache, when your heart is already aching more than you can stand? I was in the grips of real loneliness back then but I was surrounded by people all day so it never occurred to me. But loneliness is defined purely subjectively. It depends solely on whether you feel emotionally or socially disconnected from those around you. And I did."[2]

Even if there was a rational explanation for all the pain we experience, it would not exempt us from actually experiencing the pain; and that's what people are really after anyway — relief, not reasoning.

Winch was fortunate enough to connect with his brother soon after he started a downward spiral and learned his perception was not an accurate reflection of reality. However, when that doesn't happen and vulnerable people continue to believe a damaging story they invented to explain their circumstances, all manner of other things become a viable option. Too often, this is the point where people start to act out in destructive ways, because they are desperate for the comfort and validation they have not received. It's a perfect storm for addiction, and, for many vulnerable people, it becomes an unfortunate reality. Those who are able to withstand the pain of loss, without seeking refuge through destructive habits, are often forced to carry the additional burden of loneliness on their road to healing.

Researcher Naomi Eisenberger discovered that the feeling of being excluded causes loneliness. It triggers activity in the same area of the brain that registers physical pain.[3] There are many studies on loneliness to show its devastating effects such as chronic stress on the body and a compromised immune system. With this new research, we are now learning that loneliness extends beyond an unpleasant emotional state and, at least to our minds, is as real as a physical injury. Still, the way we treat people in emotional pain is often quite different from those with physical pain.

At the forefront of this problem is the simple fact that we are not as willing to acknowledge and validate emotional pain as readily as we do physical pain. If someone broke their leg, it would be absurd to pretend it was not broken. If a bone is broken, we understand that it will take time to heal before the pain will go away. We understand the injured person will need help to do their daily tasks, even the things they could previously do unassisted and without hesitation. We understand that they will eventually heal, but that healing will be a gradual process. It's no surprise that it takes a network of people to support the injured person. Additionally, we recognize the importance of having appropriate medical care. We easily acknowledge the importance of having a professional monitor the healing process and advise accordingly. People in emotional pain are not as fortunate because they can slip through the cracks a little easier than others can. Since emotional pain isn't as obvious, people can hide it better. When someone is experiencing emotional pain instead of physical pain, it is also easier for the people around them to pretend their hurt doesn't exist. Even those who are attentive and concerned may not know the severity of the pain because they cannot see it in the same way they can see a physical injury. In some cases, the person who is suffering emotionally may not have an accurate perception of reality and could be interpreting circumstances in an unhealthy manner. Regardless, the pain they feel is real to them, and they will never work through it unless it is first accepted as a legitimate issue.

After all, the key issue regarding loneliness is the rejection a person feels, and if we refuse to validate their pain, we cannot offer them much help. Since a lonely person is often afraid to ask for the help they need once they feel misunderstood, they are less inclined to share any further. They are in self-preservation mode and don't want to risk being hurt again. As a result, it becomes nearly impossible for the hurting to connect with the people in their lives who claim they are willing to help but do not give them permission to speak the truth.

Lonely people want to be connected, although there are barriers to achieving what they want, especially during a season of sorrow. When people are isolated and spend too much time by themselves, it's easy to slip into a depressive funk and become increasingly unmotivated to do anything. Without sufficient socialization, they might solely focus on the intensity of their pain and convince themselves it will never subside. Since the feeling of being disconnected is so powerful, it can distort a person's perspective by placing too much attention on their emotional needs without also seeing the hope for eventual healing. There comes a point when the pain is so great, they cannot bear it, but because they also cannot remove it, they grow increasingly numb as a way to cope with the extreme emotional overload. This numbing loneliness is a mixture of apathy and despair, a tense kind of exhaustion, and those in mourning may cycle in and out of that state until they have the energy to work through the depth of their loss.

Additionally, those willing to disclose their emotions and engage their pain might not have the capacity to invest in their relationships because they are using all their emotional energy to deal with the pervasive pain in their own lives. As bystanders, we cannot expect the bereaved to give us a list of instructions about how to help them. While it is a nice sentiment to tell a grief-ridden friend to "let us know if we can do anything" to help them, it indirectly makes them responsible for our behavior, and lets us off the hook when they are too tired to think of anything. Though we will discuss practical ways to resolve this problem in subsequent chapters, it is important for us to recognize that the way we express our concerns occasionally makes the sufferer feel like they have to alleviate their own burden.

Loneliness is rampant among the grieving, but it is an epidemic our society as a whole. We say we have friends and we think we're connected because we have all of this technology to make us feel like we are, and, in many ways, that is true. Unfortunately, there is also a downside to having so much technology at our fingertips, and, often, the very tools we use for connection make us feel increasingly disconnected. There is simply no substitute for knowing someone personally by sitting down and having a conversation with them and walking through daily life together.

Some of the loneliest people I know are very social. Like Dr. Winch, many lonely people are unaware of their loneliness because they are surrounded by people and managing other aspects of their lives quite well. Though they seem to be happy and thriving, they don't feel like anyone actually knows them. They feel alone in a crowd and keep their personal problems to themselves. When crisis hits that person's life, they don't have the capacity to start reaching out and developing a support network. If they didn't have a pre-existing network of supporters, it is likely they won't have one at all.

A disapproving attitude will shut down communication almost instantaneously, but a genuine desire to understand what someone is going through, will effortlessly establish trust.

The pains of loneliness intensify during times of distress, and many people feel the profound lack of communal support when they realize they need help and don't have anyone to lean on. Sometimes, this insight catches people by surprise because they were unaware of their friend deficit before crisis hit and are suddenly confronted with the stark reality of their aloneness in the midst of excruciating loss. As a result, lonely people often struggle with feelings of insignificance. They feel like they don't matter and assume no one cares about them or their pain, even if that is far from the truth.

Though a lack of knowledge may be driving a lack of involvement, the wounded only hear what their feelings are telling them. They only see what their friends and family aren't doing and they feel rejected and disconnected. Some start to silently resent the people in their lives because they aren't accessible to them in their time of need. Once resentment sets in, they forfeit the support many around them would happily provide if they truly understood what was needed.

When lonely people feel forgotten by their friends and family, it's easy to transfer those feelings to the spiritual realm and believe God has forgotten them too. Sometimes, we can initiate healing simply by letting someone who is suffering know we *see them*. We can also remind them that God has not abandoned them, despite evidence to the contrary. A few years ago, I was reading the story of the Exodus in the Bible when God's people were enslaved in Egypt and being horribly mistreated. I can only imagine how desperate and forgotten they must have felt, confined in an abusive situation with no conceivable hope for relief.

As I kept reading, I was struck by the significance of *remembering* and how it is directly linked to empathy. Specifically, in Exodus 3:7-8a, the Lord said, "I have surely seen the affliction of my people who are in Egypt and have heard their cry because of their taskmasters. I know their sufferings, and I have come down to deliver them out of the hand of the Egyptians and to bring them up out of that land to a good and broad land, a land flowing with milk and honey."[4] Upon further investigation, I was surprised to learn that remembering is not a passive activity. In fact, Clarke's Commentary on the Bible states, "When God *remembered* his people and how they were suffering, *it signified that he was about to act on their behalf.* His redemptive plan was about to be enacted. In other words, when God sees the afflictions of his people, his 'eye affects [his] heart.'"[5]

I wonder what our lives would look like if remembering someone's affliction actually meant we were going to do something about it. I wonder how much our hearts would expand and how much stronger our connections with the people in our lives would be if our eyes also affected our hearts. If the purpose of our remembering is so that we will empathize with those in need, each messy moment is an invitation to engage in someone else's life and become an active participant in the redemptive story God is telling in our midst.

If we want to actively remember the suffering, and increase our compassion for them, we must first be mindful of the various ways people grieve. Some people initially deal with loss better than expected and are surprised when they experience a delayed period of grief. In the beginning, though they are still hurting, they are doing as well as can be expected. Maybe these people are the ones fortunate enough to have a solid support system in place and are ahead of the healing curve, leading everyone to believe they are more resilient than is actually the case.

For others, the length of time they've been in pain is the fiercest battle. Sometimes, the longer a particular season endures, the harder it is to accept the loss. When people realize they won't ever be returning to their previous life, they might be resistant to accepting a new kind of normal. As observers, this can be confusing to us. We often think about grief, loss, and the subsequent emotional pain as a singular event. Something happened; a loved one died, lost their job, or was assaulted. Perhaps a friend discovered their spouse was having an affair or learned that their business was going under. The tragedies are as diverse as the people who live through them.

However, confusion sets in when the event that ignited the pain happened years ago and our loved ones are still dealing with the same issues. Our compassion runs out and we become intolerant to their suffering. We cannot understand why they can't "get over it" already. While there are instances where this type of prolonged grief can indeed be unhealthy, in general, we expect people to heal at a faster pace than is possible. We're impatient and want others to grieve on our timetable, but that is both unrealistic and unfair.

Grief is not as linear of a process as we like to believe it is. People can experience a loss that presents itself differently in different seasons; new losses accompany each new phase of life. Though they are mourning the same loss, they mourn it in an unfamiliar way. It may have sneaked up on them when they were least expecting it and brought with it a fresh grief, triggered by a scent or a memory or a song. Recently, a dear friend told me she is prone to having a grief relapse every time she wears one of her Nana's old scarves, because they still smell like her perfume, and it always elicits a strong emotional response.

I remember the first time I thought about grief in this manner. After a death in my family, a co-worker told me about his struggle with his father's passing many years prior. It's been several years, so I might not remember all the details correctly, but I have not forgotten the lesson. He remembered the initial grief being overwhelming and how people told him that the pain would get better with time. While his pain became less intense and he was able to accept the loss and continue healing, it never really went away. It just became more manageable. From time to time, it would resurface. At first, this surprised him because it had been years since his loss and he had worked through so much already. At this stage of his life, when he remembered his father, he was able to celebrate the time they had together and the legacy he left behind. Still, whenever he would enter into a new season of life, the grief was there, waiting for him once again. He knew how it felt to lose his father as a young man. He mourned that loss, but when he had children of his own, his grief took on a new form. He grieved for his children because they didn't know their grandfather. He grieved for himself because he couldn't call his father for advice when he had questions about how to raise his children.

He learned that each new phase of life introduced a new face of grief. Though it was confusing on the surface, once he was able to make the connections and understand it, he was able to become more compassionate toward himself when the hurt returned. It's important for us to note this facet of grief when our loved ones are struggling. The emotional strain brought on by the longevity of suffering is immense and can leave people feeling depleted and defeated. When the same old wounds resurface, it can lead to despair and hopelessness if left unchecked. It is an easy thing to overlook because the passing of time can trick us into thinking people no longer need our support or, worse yet, that they no longer deserve our support.

Occasionally, we misunderstand the root of a person's grief and become dismissive towards their suffering. Our misunderstanding, however, is not necessarily our fault. In some cases, we are confused about someone else's pain because they are confused about their own pain. In some instances, a grieving person may not know the full extent of what they are grieving. In those cases, they might need additional help to uncover the source of their pain.

If the level of grief matches the level of loss, it is generally considered to be an appropriate response.

Due to its complex nature, it is difficult to pinpoint what "healthy" grief looks like. If the level of grief matches the level of loss, it is generally considered to be an appropriate response. However, since people experience loss differently, we should use this more as a guiding principle, not as a universal fact. For example, if a person has lost someone they love, the duration of their grief will likely last a long time. Because of their profound love for the person they lost, they will probably grieve that loss, to varying degrees, for the rest of their life. In a sense, it is a tribute to a life well lived, that a person's absence is felt. Although people can also become addicted to grief or develop other unhealthy patterns that hinder the healing process, most people who have lived through an excruciating loss will simply need a long time to process their pain.

If the level of grief is disproportionate to the level of loss, it is an indication that a person might be struggling with an underlying issue, triggered by the loss, and not the loss itself. Under those circumstances, it may be helpful to gently ask probing questions related to their suffering, in order to help them identify the actual cause of their pain. Pretend you have a friend who is devastated because her boyfriend broke up with her, though they had only been dating for a short time. At first, you are compassionate because you know she was invested in the relationship and you understand it is upsetting when relationships dissolve. As time goes on, your friend remains uninterested in meeting potential new partners and continues to mourn her loss, well beyond what you feel is appropriate. Instead of discounting her pain, because you think her grief is unwarranted, you could ask follow up questions to better understand what she is feeling. By listening to your friend's responses, you may be able to help her uncover a hidden layer of grief. Perhaps she thought she was mourning a breakup, but that was only part of it. Maybe she was mourning something much deeper. What if her relationship represented all the dreams she had for her future—a future that now seems uncertain? What if she desperately wants to be a mother, and fears she will be too old to have a baby if she doesn't find a partner soon? What if she is only mildly upset about the breakup, but completely brokenhearted because she feels like her deepest longing will never be fulfilled? With that knowledge, her lingering grief might make a little more sense and evoke a little more empathy from you. As a result of engaging your friend in her grief, not only does she have more clarity but also she now has the option to confront her pain, instead of remaining stuck in her grief, perpetually wondering why she can't move on.

The work of healing is tedious; it takes time to process pain and to uncover things that have been lying dormant inside. When we rush to judgment and qualify other people's pain, we strain the bond of friendship, which leaves the bereaved feeling lonelier than ever. Fortunately, we can do better, if we're willing to put some skin in the game. There is no expiration date on compassion, and as we practice it, we become more understanding when our loved ones walk through a season of mourning.

3.

"I NEED A SAFE PLACE TO LAND"

When people find themselves in the midst of pain and confusion, it throws them into shock. Many cannot think clearly and simply react to whatever problem is most pressing at the time. During a traumatic event, a person may immediately be confronted with an onslaught of emotion. Over time, the intensity of those emotions is likely to seep into other areas of their life, without asking for consent. Emotions are loud and bossy and demand to be heard. They are both explosive and subtly pervasive, and when people we love find themselves swimming in the vastness of their emotional pain, trying to make order out of the chaos, it is easy for them to become overwhelmed.

Emotions are loud and bossy and demand to be heard. They are both explosive and subtly pervasive.

When people are in self-preservation mode, their primary concern is safety. As such, they will defend against any perceived threats, including the unintentionally hurtful things we say when we are trying to offer our support. Despite being inundated with emotional pain, the fear of rejection is so powerful that many people would rather stay silent and not risk the embarrassment an honest conversation might provoke. The fact remains, if grieving people felt safe to tell you the truth, you'd be having very different conversations than you're used to.

Wearing masks and hiding the unpleasant parts of our lives is a norm in our society, which leads those hurting to believe no one would be able to relate to their struggles. There have been many times when I have thought the same, but I have had far too many shocking conversations in recent years, to still believe it. In my experience, Henry Wadsworth Longfellow's observation, "If we could read the secret history of our enemies, we should find in each man's life sorrow and suffering enough to disarm all hostility," rings true.[1] However, we can't even read the secret history of our most esteemed friends and we don't know what we don't know. Whether we admit it or not, we all have times when we wish someone would be able to see through the façade and help us without having to ask for it. The lucky few who happen to have the type of friends who are intuitive and self-reflective might get their wish. The rest of us, who have friends who love us but cannot actually read our minds, are likely to wrestle with disappointment and resentment. When people are in pain, they need support and don't want the added pressure of having to instruct someone on how to help them because they have enough going on already. If they were honest, they'd probably tell us they don't know what they need anyway. If they were being truly honest, they'd probably tell us they feel terrified, too.

As a general rule, we like to control things. And when we are confronted with just how out of control we actually are, it is panic-inducing. It's paralyzing. Often, the first twinge of this realization during the grieving process is related to the actual loss. People realize they may have tried as hard as they could to produce a different outcome but were not able to bring it to fruition. The helplessness they feel is both maddening and heartbreaking.

But then, a secondary type of "out-of-control-ness" shows up once the immediate shock wears off. The range of emotions they feel, and, at times, the very contradictory emotions they feel, are confusing. As a result, some suppress these emotions and try to hide them from the people in their lives who could help them. And while that is a decision we cannot make for someone else, we want to do everything possible to encourage them on the path to healing and prevent them from coping with their pain in a destructive manner.

This is why it is so important that we, as supporters, do our best to create authenticity in our relationships and allow room for the unknown. When people are bombarded with so many emotions, they don't know which ones they should tend to first. They need the people in their lives to understand this and give them permission to feel their feelings, even though they might not be able to explain the complexity of what is going on inside them yet. If we create a safe haven where we embrace courage, where everyone is allowed to share their heart deeply and truthfully, we can become a catalyst for clarity and healing.

When we approach our lives and think we will be able to make sense of everything in the moment, we place undue pressure upon ourselves. In the words of Margaret Atwood, "When you are in the middle of a story it isn't a story at all, but only a confusion; a dark roaring, a blindness, a wreckage of shattered glass and splintered wood; like a house in a whirlwind, or else a boat crushed by the icebergs or swept over the rapids, and all aboard are powerless to stop it. It's only afterwards that it becomes anything like a story at all. When you are telling it, to yourself or to someone else."[2] In the middle of the experience, we just have to feel it; we have to start there. Though there's a time and place for analysis and action, we must make tending our loved one's bleeding heart a priority. Ease up on the pressure to figure it out and find a logical explanation for everything because it may not come, at least not in the timeframe we'd like it to. Even if there were a rational explanation for all the pain we experience, it would not exempt us from actually experiencing the pain; and that's what people are really after anyway—relief, not reasoning.

Plenty of people think it's their job to "toughen up" the sensitive or tell them how they should be feeling instead of simply listening to their struggles.

When someone we love is setting up camp right in the heart of the messy middle, they are likely to feel incredibly vulnerable. In those moments, one of the best things we can offer our friend is a sense of security. There's enough harshness out there and more than enough criticism to go around. Plenty of people think it's their job to "toughen up" the sensitive or tell them how they *should* be feeling instead of simply listening to their struggles. When life is unpredictable and scary, it is comforting to know there is a safe place to land. Just knowing they don't always have to have a stiff upper lip, takes the edge off, so people can let their guard down and be accepted as they actually are, not as they want to be.

In order to provide a safe space for our loved ones to grieve, we must first become a safe person. We can't expect everyone to tell us everything, and most of us know the agony of being trapped in a conversation with an over-sharer. Instead of being a dumping ground for emotional waste, we should aim to use discernment in our relationships in order to create appropriate boundaries.

Boundaries, which serve to uphold the integrity and health of both participants, help establish a loving and honest connection, where people feel secure and are willing to share the intimate details of their lives with one another. As researcher Brené Brown, wisely cautions us, "When it comes to vulnerability, connectivity means sharing our stories with people who've earned the right to hear them."[3]

What does a safe person look like? How do we become a worthy confidant, so that the suffering in our midst will identify us as their allies and seek us out in times of trouble? It's tricky because even the most insightful among us can have difficulty identifying and predicting what another person really needs. In the messy middle, people haven't had time for self-reflection. They might not be able to clearly communicate how they feel or express what they want from us because they genuinely might not know. Though we cannot be expected to be mind-readers, when time is of the essence, we don't have the luxury of waiting until we're "ready" to help. If we refuse to get involved unless we have all the information we want beforehand, we might as well wait forever.

It is more important to value sincerity over perfection in our relationships, especially in emotionally charged situations. We're all going to make mistakes and say the wrong thing every once in a while. Even the most informed person with the best intentions, will blow it on occasion. The important thing is to learn from those mistakes and keep growing, so we don't develop a pattern of poor responses but, instead, allow a few isolated incidents to teach us how to do better next time.

In my experience, one of the best ways to help people is to empathize with them. It is uncomplicated and easy to implement, because it doesn't require any answers from us. Empathy allows us to say, "I don't know what you need, but I care; and I can't make your pain go away, but I would if I could." It is the highest form of love, always willing to listen and always striving to understand.

I didn't have to agree with her perspective to understand it. I just had to be interested.

Empathy requires us to see things from someone else's perspective and enter into that experience with them. In order to understand their struggles and ease their pain, it is imperative that we reserve judgment; as Brennan Manning suggests, "The expectations of others can exert a subtle but controlling pressure on our behavior."[4] More than anything, I've found that judgment is one of the biggest hindrances to fostering a safe environment for the hurting. A disapproving attitude will shut down communication almost instantly, but a genuine desire to understand what someone is going through, will effortlessly establish trust. The importance of empathizing with one another to establish a foundation of trust in our relationships cannot be overstated; without trust, there simply is no relationship.

When I was in college, I studied acting and experienced this lesson in a deeper way than I expected. In order to prepare for my role, it required more than just saying the lines. I had to learn about my character from a first-person perspective. I had to be present with her and learn to think the way she did. My director would encourage us to develop an entire story about our character's life. In order to be clear and appreciate the journey our characters were about to embark on, we'd have to uncover their motivations and ways of being in the world. It wasn't enough to know what my character did; I needed to know why she did it. I needed to know her history and how she interpreted things in order to fully appreciate her story. I had to find something relatable in my character in order to play the role honestly. I couldn't articulate it at the time, but what I was really searching for was her humanity; and that is the goal of our relationships off stage as well. It's amazing what happens when we make understanding and relatability a focal point. In acting, it allowed me to be more compassionate toward my character and not judge her for her flaws. I had to develop a story about her to give me context about who she was and what she wanted. I didn't have to agree with her perspective to understand it. I just had to be interested.

In our relationships off stage, I find the willingness to learn about the whole person to be equally as critical. In order to understand the people we love, we have to be interested in their stories. Who are they? What have they been through? How do they make sense of their world? We have to think of them as dynamic people, filled to the brim with intricate layers and depth and weird associations and unique experiences. Unfortunately, we often overlook the complexity of a person's struggles because we assume things are more clear-cut than they are.

When we carry a black-and-white mentality with us into crisis, we forget about the gray parts. As a result, when we try to help the hurting, we forget that each individual interprets things through their own unique lens. Therefore, each individual will walk their own unique path toward wholeness. People think the way they do for a reason; they didn't get there by accident. Rather, the way they think, feel, and behave is rooted in something. That's not to say it's always rooted in the truth, but there are legitimate reasons behind their views and emotions. If we are unwilling to consider what those things are, then we will be ill equipped to help.

If we truly desire to be of help in a time of need, it is necessary to first look for the humanity of the person instead of passing judgment about how appropriately we feel they are dealing with their pain. If we don't know where to begin, we can start by asking clarifying questions in place of judgmental evaluations. Instead of thinking we already know what's going on in someone else's mind, we can be curious and compassionate. For example, a judgmental person might see the problems in a friend's relationship and remark, "She wouldn't be in this mess if she would stop going out with losers," but an empathetic person might wonder, "Why does she feel unworthy to date a quality man?" Neither response forces it's participants to be in agreement about the situation or hide their true feelings. However, one response addresses the problem in a way that shuts down communication, whereas the other promotes understanding and honest reflection about the root of the problem.

Depending on the level of self-awareness in an individual and their openness to share their insights with us, we might have an easier time initiating conversation and discerning which kind of response is most needed from us in their time of pain. But, it is common for both sides to be oblivious to at least some things that are going on inside themselves. After all, we are always on a path of self-discovery. It only complicates the process when one person thinks their way is the only way and tries to force their expectations on the other.

The manner in which this "my way or the highway" attitude presents itself in crisis is especially dangerous because it often goes unnoticed by the caregiver. Often, people want to help, so they help in the best way they know how. Yet, sometimes, even though we think we are being supportive, we are not being supportive in the way the person needs us to be. There is a disconnect. As we discussed in the previous chapter, when people feel misunderstood, the relational bond is threatened. We could unintentionally be creating barriers in our relationships that make it harder for our friends to heal. We may think we are being very supportive when, in reality, we've just unknowingly wounded our friends.

In order to provide a safe place for the grieving, we must lead with empathy not advice.

For example, let's pretend we have a friend who is going through a divorce and we want to be supportive. When we see our friend, instead of asking how they are coping with this loss, we offer up a verbal highlight reel of their ex's worst moments. We think we're being a great friend because we generally care and have their best interests in mind, but we never stopped to consider how it might feel to be on the receiving end of our "help."

Perhaps, we've just made our friend feel even worse. In addition to feeling the vast range of emotional pain related to the divorce, now they also feel stupid. Maybe they even feel like we are judging them for being stupid. If their ex was such an obviously horrible person, why did it take them so long to notice? Why did they marry them in the first place? Why are they even upset about the end of the relationship? After all, if they're better off without their ex, it doesn't make sense to be so emotional about parting ways. In this example, the desire to affirm our friend's value and give them what we think they need (by speaking ill about their ex), feels dismissive towards their very real grief, in the wake of betrayal, years lost, and unrequited love.

While our opinion about their ex could be completely valid, that is not the issue at hand. There will likely come a point where our friend will have to ask themselves some hard questions and do the internal work necessary for healing. We may or may not play a key role in that process. However, what our friends' crave most in crisis, is for us to reaffirm our relationship with them. They need to know our bond of friendship is secure enough to allow them the freedom to be who they are, and feel how they feel, without being judged for it. They need to know we understand there will be other losses tied up in the initial loss, so we won't be dismissive toward their pain, but will be patient enough to endure the mess until things get a little less messy.

We can learn to become more compassionate and helpful in times of crisis the way we learn to do most things. We take baby steps; we practice and we start to value connection over clarity. In order to provide a safe place for the grieving, we must lead with empathy not advice, and we must embody the character traits of a safe person. Once we become a person others can trust with their pain, we become an ally for their healing.

4.

"WOULD YOU BE KIND AND HOLD OUT YOUR HAND?"

I find there is usually a breakdown between what we want to do and how we actually implement it. Several common mistakes we make when we are concerned for our loved ones experiencing loss are interconnected. What I am going to say next is going to seem counterintuitive, but trust me on this one. It's going to come in handy, especially if you find yourself caring for someone who is experiencing prolonged grief. I've learned this lesson the hard way.

You need to prioritize your own self-care. Enlist a group of people who you can lean on for help when you need it because, at some point, you will need it. Support groups, friends, and professionals are just as important for the caregiver's well-being as those experiencing the loss firsthand. You cannot continue to give without also being replenished, or you will become depleted and unable to help anyone else. If your goal is to help your friend heal, you are setting yourself up for failure if you choose to ignore your own health.

You may feel guilty for taking time to focus on your own well-being, especially when you compare it to the depth of your loved one's need. However, you must take care of yourself in the process or you will get burned out. If you allow yourself to get to that point, you will not have anything left to offer anyone else. Intense involvement in someone else's pain without proper self-care could also cause you to resent the very people you're trying to help, because you feel overextended and emotionally drained. Some people eventually develop "compassion fatigue," which I didn't know was a real thing until I started researching the subject for this book. Though I've heard the term used before, and I certainly understand its sentiment, I had no idea it was a common, diagnosable condition.

While it is natural and honorable to desire to help someone we love, we have to take care of ourselves in the process so that we are truly capable of providing such help, or it could easily backfire on us.

Compassion fatigue is more than just a colloquial term we use to express our level of disconnectedness to the pain around us; it is actually a secondary form of post-traumatic stress that clinicians and caregivers commonly experience due to the emotional intensity of their work. In his educational video, *When Helping Hurts: Sustaining Trauma Workers,* Dr. Frank M. Ochberg says, "Everyone who moves toward the scene to help, everyone who comforts someone who was there, everyone who listens closely, with sensitivity, is a potential casualty. But every one of us is also a source of comfort, information and inspiration."[1] While it is natural and honorable to desire to help someone we love, we have to take care of ourselves in the process so that we are truly capable of providing such help, or it could easily backfire on us.

On the other hand, sometimes, we struggle because we recognize our limitations and are afraid to enforce appropriate boundaries. We may choose to make ourselves more available to a friend than we typically would simply because they genuinely need it and we genuinely care. I'm all for that. Yet, we must recognize that when we say "yes" to one thing, we also need to say "no" to other things, or we're going to be very imbalanced.

Making personal sacrifices in order to be a supportive friend is a wonderful gift. We all need people like that, and I'm certainly grateful for those who have been willing to do it for me. However, if we're going to be investing our time, emotions, and maybe even finances at a heightened level of care, it is important to assess our other obligations. We'll have to cut some things out that are not the priority for a particular season, or enlist the help of others who can pick up our slack while we're tending to the bereaved. For example, you decide you're going to prepare extra food and spend a few hours visiting your grief-stricken friend one night a week for a month. However, your schedule is already very full and you usually spend time each week driving your children around to soccer practice. In order to ease the load, you could ask a friend to share your chauffeuring responsibilities until you are able to commit to your regular schedule again. Then, you will be able to invest the time you would have spent driving, into your relationship with your hurting friend, without the added pressure of trying to find more free hours in your day.

Boundaries exist to protect relationships not destroy them. By using wisdom in establishing a healthy routine for yourself, you are setting yourself up for relational success, even during periods of loss.

Maintaining boundaries does not mean we are bad friends. There will likely be times in the healing process when our friends will ask us to give them more than we have to give, or perhaps more than we are willing to give. Just because somebody wants something from us does not mean they are entitled to it. We do not need to throw away healthy boundaries because someone is in pain and would welcome more care than we are able to give them at that time. We can still be involved, caring, and helpful, even if we cannot devote all of our time and energy towards our loved one's healing.

Also, it is important to remind ourselves of our role. We are there to be a friend and offer support. We don't have to pretend we are therapists if we are not. There's no need to make up a diagnosis or suggest a course of action if we aren't trained to do so because there are professionals who can fill that space in their lives. When we free ourselves from having to know what to do at every moment, we allow ourselves to walk with them through the pain without undue pressure. We all have times in our lives when things are overwhelming and will require additional support to get through. However, just like we can offer varying degrees of support, we also offer distinctly different types of support, depending on our strengths.

Sometimes, we have an image in our head about what it means to be supportive, but that doesn't mean it's a one size fits all kind of deal. We have to be sensitive to our friend's needs and personalities before we assume we know what to do. Consider the types of things you are good at and see if there is a way to use those skills or interests to assist. We will explore practical ways to implement this throughout the rest of the book, but for now, just remember there is no "right" way to do this.

By all means, invest wholeheartedly and be a support to your grieving friend, just don't pretend you are a superhero in the process. That doesn't help anyone. If you have the support you need, you will be able to be supportive when your friends need to rely on you more than they ever thought they would. Boundaries exist to protect relationships not destroy them. By using wisdom in establishing a healthy routine for yourself, you are setting yourself up for relational success, even during periods of loss.

Still, sometimes, when we see our limitations, we feel so badly because we can't do everything, we end up doing nothing at all. We feel as though the little we have to contribute will not make a difference. We downplay our role in our friends' lives and the impact we can make even in the harshest of circumstances. We bear a burden we cannot carry because we feel we are responsible to remove someone else's pain, but we cannot.

It's not an easy thing to accept, but there are times in our lives, no matter how much we wish we could change reality, we simply cannot. And that leaves us feeling like we are unnecessary. We compare the magnitude of someone's pain to the limited amount of help we can offer, and render ourselves useless. We think the little we have to give is so insignificant that it will not help or even be noticed by someone in pain. So, we remove ourselves all together because we think we have nothing to offer anyway.

In some instances, we recognize the value of our contributions and we shy away from helping because we think the person in need will bleed us dry. We know we have a limited about of resources, but we still want to help. We can't do everything, but we can do something. But, we fear that if our friend knows we are willing to help, we will be taken advantage of and become the point person for every need that arises. In the wake of a tragedy, it is easy for us to excuse ourselves from playing an active role in the healing process if we are convinced there are plenty of other people who can help. If we decide we aren't needed, it doesn't seem like such a bad thing to express our condolences and simultaneously keep our distance.

It's amazing how a simple hug has an acute way of communicating exactly what is necessary during the hardest moments of our lives.

Once we have the proper boundaries in place and people ready to support us when we need it, we're ready to shift our focus on helping our loved one. The goal is simple: Aim to be the kind of person who is so kind and generous Natalie Merchant would have to write a song about you. That is the type of friend everyone wants in a crisis. Start by thinking about practical needs and address those first. Can you organize a group of people willing to prepare food? Drive them to the doctor? Pick up their children from school? Do the laundry? Surely, there are many things to choose from.

As we discussed earlier, our responsibilities do not magically disappear just because we don't have the stamina to keep up with them in a crisis. While helping with these practical tasks may not be glamorous or ease emotional pain, it is still helpful. Eliminating even one thing from the monstrous pile of things to do, will make a felt difference. Also, it's amazing how a simple hug has an acute way of communicating exactly what is necessary during the hardest moments of our lives. The best part is, they are easy to give and don't require any insights or explanations to be effective.

Additionally, I've found a simple way to remain involved, especially over prolonged periods, is to ask follow-up questions. If we know someone is having a rough time but we never say anything about it, they're going to think we don't care. This is especially true if we've talked about their pain in detail and then never bring it up again. They will not feel free to bring it up in future conversations if we've been distant or unresponsive. When someone bares their soul and it is met with seeming disregard or disinterest, it makes them feel a heightened sense of insecurity. It's common for them to silently wonder why we don't care and for them to make up an entire catalog of reasons we are not behaving the way they expect.

When someone bares their soul and it is met with seeming disregard or disinterest, it makes them feel a heightened sense of insecurity.

In reality, one of the biggest reasons we don't ask follow-up questions is because we don't know if our friend wants us to keep bringing it up. We don't want to reinjure someone we love, and we fear that we may hurt them more by mentioning it again. Since we don't want to trigger that response, we avoid it altogether. However, our lack of attention can also trigger responses we don't want, though we might not be privy to that knowledge. Privately, our friends might think we've forgotten about them, are self-absorbed, or insensitive to their very present need.

Since this is not what we're going for, how do we remedy it? I've found a few approaches to be particularly effective. First, when someone shares their story with you, validate it. Acknowledge you've heard them and thank them for being willing to share. Don't take it lightly; it's a big deal when someone trusts you with their pain. Then, follow up with them over time and check in to see how they are doing. Ask them how they are feeling and remind them you haven't forgotten about them. It's astounding how many people feel forgotten, but it's comforting to learn someone truly sees you.

If this kind of exchange does not come naturally to you, that's okay. The more you do it, the more comfortable it will become. You will probably make some mistakes, but that is simply part of learning. Just be sincere and interested in hearing their story, and give yourself permission to do it awkwardly at first. If you are afraid to keep asking them how they are doing because you don't want to upset them, tell them so. Ask them if you are hurting them by talking about their loss and be willing to refrain from asking questions if they're not interested in having a conversation about it. Extend the invitation for them to share with you if they feel it would be beneficial and let them determine the tone of your interactions.

If talking about emotional trauma makes you feel uncomfortable, tell them. Tell them how you want them to know you care, but don't always know how to express it because you are nervous. We try so hard to be mind readers and guess what we should do, but we make things harder than they need to be when we are too afraid to admit how we feel and won't communicate with one another honestly. So much guesswork could be eliminated if we were willing to have difficult but necessary conversations, in order to create the type of depth and trust to sustain our relationships in times of crisis.

5.

"YOU DON'T HAVE TO FIND THE WORDS TO SAY"

Ask anyone experiencing relational problems what went awry and you'll inevitably hear the predictable answer: communication. Why is it that something we all recognize as a pillar of a strong relationship, something we do all day, every day, is so difficult to do well? You'd think we would have mastered the art of communication eons ago and easily interact with each other, given all that we know about it and how frequently we practice it.

However, intellectual knowledge and practical implementation of said knowledge are two different things entirely. If we spent a little time digging around the perimeters of our relationships, we would undoubtedly find more under the surface than we'd ever imagine. I studied communication when I was in college and I'll always remember how my favorite professor would react to this phenomenon. She told us how people occasionally had unrealistic expectations about her interpersonal communications simply because she spent so much time analyzing it. As though being an expert in the field somehow exempted her from the everyday problems we all experience. While I can attest that she was quite a skilled communicator, she assured us she has all the same challenges the rest of us have. She had to "practice what she preached" in order to become the effective communicator she is, because knowing about something did not magically give her the ability to perfectly execute what she learned. "Just because a person studies math, doesn't mean they are the number seven," she remarked, "and just because we study communication doesn't mean we communicate perfectly."[1]

Communication is so much more than the words we speak; it's as much what we say as what we don't say.

Learning to communicate how we feel and listening attentively to our friends and family members is a process. We all need opportunities to practice and hone our skills. Fortunately, we have an endless stream of opportunities to do that every single day. Communication is so much more than the words we speak; it's as much what we say as what we don't say. In fact, some studies claim nonverbal communication accounts for as much as 93% of all communication.[2] (Though the consensus among many researchers is that our nonverbal communication is in the 60-75% range.) If this is true, then there is a lot we can do to express ourselves and our support for our loved ones without even formulating a word. Words are important and they hold a lot of power, so I'm not suggesting you get a free pass and will never have to talk about your feelings or listen to someone else share theirs. Nice try, though. Sometimes, however, we get hung up on the words, especially in the wake of a tragedy. They trip us up because we aren't quite sure what to say or when we should say it. When we see someone going through something difficult, we usually feel the impulse to say *something*. Since that's the place we get into trouble rather quickly, I want to help you out. On behalf of all of those you care about who are grieving, I am giving you permission to say absolutely nothing.

You do not have to show up with a list of answers or explanations for a pain you can neither understand nor change. You do not have to find a way to make everything better, because it is likely you will not. Your main priority is simply to show up, to care. Be willing to sit in the silence when the answers do not come. Be empathetic when the "not yet" feels like it's going to be a "not ever," because those moments are going to present themselves at some point, and the way you respond to them is going to be permanently etched into your friend's brain. It will determine whether they see you as a source of comfort and run to you for support, or as an adversary to their healing and run away from you to protect their heart from further hurt.

Perhaps nothing communicates this point quite as effectively as this quote by Chuck Colson: "Our presence in a place of need is more powerful than 1,000 sermons."[3] Though advice and instructions are often useful, it requires wisdom to discern when it's appropriate to share and when it's appropriate to be quiet. What hurting people want most from us is our being present with them. They're not looking for our advice or plans or pity. They want to know we see them, care about them, and hurt with them too. Frequently, we feel the responsibility to speak when we have nothing to say. In all likelihood, we are also grieving the same loss as our friend, to a lesser degree, and may have a host of unanswered questions ourselves.

You do not have to show up with a list of answers or explanations for a pain you can neither understand nor change.

Several years ago, I went to India and experienced the healing power of presence in a new way. A few of my friends and I were there visiting and working alongside our friends who pastored a church in town. The purpose of our trip was less about accomplishing a project and more about building relationships and helping wherever there was a need. Once we arrived, we were asked to put together an event for a number of widows from the church. Though we were happy to do so, we also felt extremely ill-prepared. What could *we,* who have lead comparatively cushy lives, possibly tell *them,* who had lived through things we could not even imagine?

We were in high spirits and excited to get to know the women in attendance, but we also faced some unexpected challenges. Thankfully, our day was broken up into two sessions: morning and afternoon. That structure, combined with music, was our saving grace. We prepared a bunch of material for our time together, but went through everything much faster than we had anticipated. Naturally, we started to panic a little. I would get up and sing another song to give us something to do and buy us a few more minutes to think about what else we were going to do after I finished the song. We were enjoying our time together, but we were not sure the widows would've been able to say the same. A few highlights of the morning session included several of the ladies spitting out the candy we gave them as a gift as well as accidentally starting a small fire that *almost* got out of control. During our break for lunch, we were talking amongst ourselves, sure that the widows hated us and thought we were a bunch of idiots. If they actually were thinking that, we didn't really have much of a rebuttal. Nonetheless, our hearts were in the right place, and we wanted to help. We kept trying to find a way to connect with each other, but it seemed like there were too many obstacles in the way.

One of my friends suggested we change things up for the afternoon session, and I did not need further convincing. Since we didn't speak the same language, conversation was hard. But our dear friend, Julie, served as our translator. We decided we would start the second session by sharing our stories. No agenda or wrapping it up at the end of the day with a three-step program to improve their lives. We were just a bunch of women sitting around, sharing about things we've been through and what was going on in our lives at the time. We went first. Then, we asked the ladies to do the same.

Each time the melody changes tone, or the tempo, the harmony must follow along, or it will not sound good.

One by one, we went around the circle and shared our stories of heartbreak and hope. In the moment, I had no idea what they were saying, but somehow the lack of common words actually increased the bond between us all. Julie would graciously recap what was said, so we all could understand the gist of everyone's story. Though each woman spoke in a language I could not recognize, I was forced deeper into the moment. I had to first pay attention to the emotion behind what they were saying, instead of accepting that the words were the whole story.

I still remember those stories. One woman shared about her husband who had left on a business trip shortly after they were married and never returned. She never knew if he walked out on her or if he was killed on his travels. She has been waiting for an answer to that question for about 35 years now. Another sweet lady said she prayed her handicapped son would die before her, because she feared he would be abused by other family members and others in the community once she was no longer alive to intervene on his behalf. Still another, stricken with fresh grief after the sudden passing of her husband, could only utter a few words before her tears interrupted her.

Every person had a turn to share whatever they wanted while the rest of us sat and listened. We cried. We hugged. We prayed. Then, we thanked everyone for sharing. But we had nothing else to say. There were no quick fixes or pretending things were going to magically get better overnight. Yet, every person in the room felt loved; we all left feeling better than we did when we arrived.

Once we were able to get out of our own way and give ourselves permission to listen without an agenda, another world opened up right before our eyes. Because we were free not to give an answer, we were allowed to give our hearts. Much like life, the time we shared was beautiful and vulnerable and unpredictable. Despite a rough start, we laughed and cried and formed unlikely friendships. To this day, it reminds me how healing just showing up can be.

How do we know when we should say something and when we should not? There's no foolproof way to tell. It requires discernment because people in grief experience so many emotions simultaneously, and, as a result, their emotional state can fluctuate drastically. We don't have to be mind readers, but if we pay attention, we'll be able to pick up on a few clues.

Adrianne Haslet-Davis is a dancer who lost her leg during the bombing at the Boston Marathon in 2013. Her tenacity and optimism are inspiring, and her honesty about her struggles after losing a limb, are a rare gift to those of us who have the privilege to learn from her. Like many people who have lived through a traumatic event, she experienced additional challenges as she grieved, based in part on the way some people responded to her immediately afterwards. In her TED talk, "What people say when they don't know what to say," Haslet-Davis advises us to "take the temperature of the room," before we say a word.[4] We gauge the temperature to decide how we should dress, so why not do the same emotionally? When we visit a friend in pain, we need to be aware of their mood and respond appropriately. If they are angry, validate their feelings of anger. If they are crying, don't hold back your tears. Whatever they are feeling, authenticate their experience and sit in it with them. They will likely swing from one end of the emotional spectrum to the other at different points along their journey. That is normal during a season of loss, so don't even worry about trying to figure things out. The figuring out part will come later, and what is most needed is the connection only the gift of presence can bring.

Once, I heard Joy Williams say, "All harmony is active listening."[5] While we apply this more commonly to musicianship, I think it is fitting in our relationships as well. Musically, this refers to the relationship between various tones on scale. Interpersonally, harmony is defined, among other things, as "agreement" and "accord."[6] When we are caring for our friends and their hearts are breaking, we need to actively listen to the emotional notes they're playing (the melody).

Even if our message is appropriate or helpful, if our delivery is insensitive, the person on the receiving end may not even hear our point.

Once we distinguish which notes they are playing, and not before, then we are free to choose the appropriate notes to add, as well as the proper timing in which to add them (harmony). The melody drives the relationship; it is the focus. The harmony adds depth and intrigue to make the melody stronger. When played together, all the distinct tones that collectively make up the chord, create something beautiful.

However, it is their relationship to each other that determines whether the notes will be pleasing or not. A melody line is comprised of many notes. Each time the melody changes the tone, or the tempo, the harmony must follow along, or it will not sound good. It's an active kind of listening, the kind that offers a note at just the right time but is clear that its strength is utilized best in a supporting role.

This is the mindset we should all aspire to have when caring for the brokenhearted. We are there to serve them in the best way possible, not to run the show. We do not dictate how that will happen or even set the pace. We are the responders. When I'm trying to help and can't find the words, I find comfort in the words of Maya Angelou, knowing "people will forget what [I] said, people will forget what [I] did, but people will never forget how [I] made them feel."[7] Every once in a while, we say something so profound it lodges itself into a person's memory and they never forget it, but those moments are few and far between. More often than not, people will not be able to recall exactly what we said. They'll just remember if it made them want to share more or shut down.

How we communicate with people who are emotionally fragile is of utmost importance. Even if our message is appropriate or helpful, if our delivery is insensitive, the person on the receiving end may not even hear our point. I've experienced this firsthand. Several years ago, I would have the same old fight with one of my friends. I am a sensitive person and he was very abrasive, though he did not see how his communication style was hurting many people he interacted with, including me. Instead, he thought of himself as a very straightforward, matter-of-fact type. I think he thought he was actually helping people overcome their *sensitivity problem* by beating it out of them or teaching them how to toughen up. He did not see the connection between the way he communicated with others and their reactions to him. As far as he was concerned, they were not interrelated at all. As far as I was concerned, there was a direct correlation between the two.

So we'd fight. ALL. THE. TIME. He'd say, "You just have to be *brutally honest*." and I would say, "You can be honest *without being a brute*." And around and around we'd go. He was never able to make the connection, at least, not during the time that I knew him. Eventually, many of the people in his life grew tired of it and moved on, which was unfortunate, because there were many times I think he really wanted to help people, and, many times, he had legitimate concerns and contributions. However, no one was able to receive it. They couldn't hear what he was saying because of the way in which he said it. Sometimes, that is how we act when we are trying to be supportive. We might be well intentioned, but if we do not give thought to how the person on the receiving end might feel, it could end in disaster. If we wound them in the delivery of the message, they will only remember the additional pain we inflicted, not our point. But, if we've taken the temperature of the room and are listening for the right moment to share something that's been on our mind, we don't have to be afraid to talk about it. If we have a gentle spirit, people will usually be receptive to hearing what we have to say.

It is possible to be honest and nonthreatening, but it is not common.

I promise, it is possible to be honest and nonthreatening, but it is not common. As we learn to be more sensitive and discerning, this will gradually become easier. The more comfortable we become with silence, the less we will speak as a way to alleviate our personal discomfort and the more we will recognize when speaking is appropriate and helpful. The more we practice these disciplines, the more our instincts will guide us in the direction we need to go. Then, when the opportunity to share presents itself, we will not fear it. Instead of causing unintentional harm, we will be able to use our words to aid in the healing process.

6.

"WE DON'T ALWAYS KNOW IF WE'RE GOING TO BE OKAY"

We do a disservice to our friends when we try to predict a future we don't control. If someone tells us a heartbreaking story, it's important to take some time to let it sink in. Those of us who are natural encouragers might instinctively want to comfort people by reassuring them of a positive outcome. While I am never one to discourage a hopeful attitude, even our optimism must be paired with sensitivity when we are interacting with the bereaved. I liken this concept to the warning given in Proverbs 27:14, which says, "A loud and cheerful greeting early in the morning will be taken as a curse."[1] I'm a night owl through and through, so that verse makes me incredibly happy for obvious reasons. In the same way that I don't want anyone to talk to me before I've had ample time to drink my morning coffee, someone who is grieving does not want to listen to our ill-timed cheeriness in the wake of their sorrow. Though it sounds crazy, we can actually wound people with our optimism. It's great to be a voice of inspiration and bring the bright light of hope into the darkness. Were it not for the encouragers in my own life, I would have been swallowed up into the abyss of despair many times myself.

Our good intentions and positivity are honorable and welcomed at the appropriate time, but when people experience loss, we have to be careful not to let our hopefulness prompt us to make promises we can't keep.

Though it sounds crazy, we can actually wound people with our optimism.

When our loved one is hurting and we want to be able to remove their pain, we'll find ourselves searching for something, anything, to say in an attempt to alleviate their pain, even if nothing really seems to fit. In those moments, we should listen and embrace the silence. For most of us, however, the awkwardness of silence leads to our downfall and we inevitably open our mouths. We rack our brains, trying to think of something, and, when we can't, we revert back to things we've heard other people say in difficult moments because we're fresh out of original material. Eventually, we find ourselves in the midst of a conversation, rattling off some cliché we've heard a million times because it's the first thing that comes to mind.

Honestly, is there anything more annoying than someone trying to get you to "look on the bright side" of a devastating loss before you've even had time to process what happened? People are known to say the craziest things in these moments, leaving the person their comments are directed towards trying to absorb the shock as best they can. Having an unintentionally flippant attitude about a serious heartache, feels insensitive and even repulsive to the person struggling. Imagine your child died and someone said, "At least you're young. You can always have another baby." Would that make you feel better?

Sometimes the worst offenders are the people who most want the wounded to know how loved they are, despite their circumstances.

Or suppose you invested the last 20 years of your life developing a team or a product for a company you love, only to get laid off because the economy tanked. Instead of living the cushy life you envisioned, you're now working at a coffee shop, earning minimum wage, and hoping the bank doesn't foreclose on your house. Then, someone you know walks in and orders a latte. On their way out the door, they tell you they're sure things are going to turn around for you and not to worry because "everything happens for a reason." Would you feel like that person understood what you were going through?

Perhaps you're single and desperately want to be married, but despite your best efforts to find someone, every night you go home to an empty house. Though you have an active social life and a thriving career, you still wish you had a life partner and wrestle with loneliness and unfulfilled dreams. Then, your happily married friend sees you, dateless, at another friend's wedding, and insists that "you'll find someone when you least expect it." Would that feel reassuring?

Given all the inappropriate things we say to people in the name of being helpful, it's truly a wonder they don't punch us right in the face. We tell people with cancer that "God will never give them more than they can handle," as their hair falls out from the chemo and their bodies grow increasingly frail. We tell the distraught widow that "God works all things together for good," as she buries the love of her life and scrambles to create a semblance of normalcy for her fatherless children. Then, we tell ourselves that those words are a source of comfort to the suffering, and that is a big problem.

Sometimes the worst offenders are the people who most want the wounded to know how loved they are, despite their circumstances. In the midst of overwhelming pain, many people seek refuge in their communities of faith. Even people who've never been interested in God and aren't sure if they believe in God often run to the Church for comfort and hope. As a person of faith, I wholeheartedly support that decision, but I can't tell you how many times we've dropped the ball on this one. As demonstrated in the stories above, the things Christians say to people during their worst moments is astounding.

For example, you may sincerely believe "God works all things together for good," but that does not implicitly make all things good. Horrible things happen every day, and though I wish it were not true, suffering is an unavoidable part of the world in which we live. However, God is not the giver of tragedy and He is not indifferent towards our pain. In the Garden of Eden, we see God's original design for our world. He intended us to live in perfect harmony with Him and with each other, but because genuine love requires freedom of choice, He also gave us permission to make our own decisions. We get to decide if we will help or hinder, love or hate. Unfortunately, we live in a broken world and do not always make good choices. As a result, we suffer the consequences of our actions, or are victimized by someone else's poor choices. If we also consider everything we cannot control, such as accidents, natural disasters, and disease, the list of traumas a person could potentially endure grows exponentially.

Even so, I believe everything that happens to us is first filtered through the sovereign hand of God, although I do not completely understand how it works, and struggle to comprehend why He sometimes permits truly awful things to happen. While I also believe He is willing and able to redeem the painful moments of our lives, I'm not going to pretend I know how He'll do it. To the grieving, it can feel callous to speculate why God allowed something heinous to occur or what He is planning to bring about as the result of their loss. It makes it seem as though their pain is not a big deal to God, which is not a particularly comforting sentiment. Additionally, it undermines their experience, as our words can make them feel like their very real emotional pain is exaggerated or unwarranted. It's also noteworthy to consider that our go-to phrase, "God works all things together for good," is not a complete thought, but only a fragment of the verse in which it is contained. The second half of the verse, "to those who love God, to those who are called according to His purpose," speaks to even more complex theological issues, which for the purposes of this book, I will not address further. Moreover, we're prone to overlook another crucial element of the verse—the part that says *God*, Himself, will work it out for good, not *us*. When I hear this passage misused, I can't help but think of Anne Lamott's hilarious, yet profound, insight—that the difference between us and God is "God doesn't think He's [us]."[2]

While I also believe He is willing and able to redeem the painful moments of our lives, I'm not going to pretend I know how He'll do it.

After a tragedy in our congregation, my childhood pastor reminded us that "we live by promises, not explanations."[3] When I find myself tempted to draw conclusions about something I don't know anything about, I often remember a story about the Israelites wandering in the wilderness, not long after God parted the Red Sea. Though they witnessed a miracle and walked through the sea on dry land, they soon found themselves wandering around the desert without water. When they eventually found a spring, its water was bitter, so God used Moses to perform another miracle and made the water sweet. They continued wandering and eventually camped at a place called Elim, which was like an oasis because it had twelve springs and seventy palm trees.[4] As I read this story, I was struck by the additional commentary in my Bible, which said, "It signified to Israel once again that, since the LORD is leading them, they should not conclude too quickly that they know the meaning of their circumstances, especially when they cannot yet see how the Lord will work on their behalf (e.g., parting the Red Sea)."[5] I believe it would also serve us well to heed the same advice.

In their defense, most of the people who say these horrible things are actually trying to help, though it's not an excuse for insensitivity. If you've been the person who's rattled off one of these platitudes in a crisis, you're in good company. Most of us have been unknowingly flippant towards someone else's pain at one point or another, especially if we have faith in a God who is as loving and powerful as He says He is. When we've seen God transform our own mess and read about the miraculous stories in the Bible, it motivates us to hope, even when we feel hopeless. Because we sincerely believe everything will be okay, at least in the ultimate sense, we feel compelled to share that truth when people are in the pit of despair. The problem is that even though we believe God will one day redeem and restore, it is not going to stop people from feeling. Nothing we say or do will remove their grief or make them forget what happened. As Rowan Williams profoundly reminds us, "Grace will remake but not undo. There is all the difference in the world between Christ uncrucified and Christ risen."[6]

When we spend our time focusing on the theology of suffering but refuse to enter into the fellowship of suffering, we miss the point entirely.

When we spend our time focusing on the theology of suffering but refuse to enter into the fellowship of suffering, we miss the point entirely. Unless we are willing to sit with the brokenhearted and "weep with those who weep," our earnest desire to comfort and encourage them will not be felt.[7] Once we acknowledge the tension that exists between what a person cognitively believes to be true and emotionally feels to be true, we will communicate more gracefully with those who are overwhelmed by their loss. Moreover, our faith does not restrict us from expressing sorrow. Real faith is the freedom to express everything we feel and know God can handle it—which is why it might be better to skip the clichés and respond in a more genuine way. For instance, you could say something like this:

"I don't know why this happened to you and if I could

change things, I would. I don't know what to say, because I know nothing I say will take away your pain; but I want you to know that I care. Even though it might not feel like it right now, God promises He is near to the brokenhearted; so, I am asking Him to draw near to you. His name is 'Immanuel,' the God who is 'with us,' even in the worst of times.[8] He specializes in helping people who are desperate and hopeless and He is big enough to handle your pain. He's even big enough to handle the disappointment you feel because He didn't intervene in the way you had hoped. You're allowed to be honest, and sad, and angry, and your cries are not falling on deaf ears. He hears you and so do I. I'm committed to do whatever I can to help you through this, and I'm praying God will do what I cannot."

Real faith is the freedom to express everything we feel and know God can handle it.

Like a glass falling to the floor, when someone's life is shattered, it breaks into many little pieces. There are sharp edges and when you look at the aftermath it's hard to recognize what it looked like before it broke. When you start to clean up the mess, you might get cut if you're not careful. You might even find shards of glass in places you didn't expect and it will make you wonder "How did that get all the way over here?" Those suffering great loss often feel like the damage they've sustained is beyond repair, and, to some degree, they are right. Though the tragedy they experienced does not define them, it is forever a defining moment in their lives. It shapes them, for better or for worse, and though a wonderful life is possible post-tragedy, it is unlikely that the new life will be an exact replica of the old one. In an instant, their world shifted, and they're left to find the remaining the pieces of themselves and the life they once knew scattered all over the ground. Then we come along and tell them that, "it's going to be okay" as if that miraculously changes everything. No matter what happens in their future, they will be a different person as a result of the trauma than they were going into it. When we tell people they'll be fine, when they know their lives will never, ever be the same again, it doesn't sit well. We interrupt their healing by refusing to let them ask uncomfortable questions and share their fears. They need to know it's "okay not to be okay" when they are afraid and don't know what the outcome will be.

In my own life, I've found these heart-wrenching moments to be necessary for my long-term emotional well-being. Though it seems counterintuitive, those times can be a catalyst for healing because that is the point where the hurting person is fed up. They don't have any energy left to pretend they believe things they don't. They get real and start to own how they feel, even if it's not pretty. They question what they truly believe. They might get really angry or depressed. They ask "why?" But they don't receive a satisfying answer and probably never will.

To go through something traumatic and not have an emotional reaction is a sign that something is off.

When our loved ones experience the intensity of their emotions and question everything they previously thought to be true, we do not have to panic because that is normal. It's awful, but it's normal. To go through something traumatic and not have an emotional reaction is a sign that something is off. If a person was in any way attached to something or someone, and it dies or changes in a drastic way, it's going to hurt, and they will need to mourn the loss, or they will be paralyzed by it forever. It's bound to shake things up and bring things to the surface they might not have even known were there. How they respond and, for that matter, how we respond, will set the tone. If they are willing to ask the tough questions and acknowledge their fears and doubts, then they will, at least, have a place to start. They'll know what is hardest for them to understand and accept, and they'll be able to confront those issues with the help of friends or a trained professional.

Still, when things change so dramatically, many people find themselves longing for the way things were in the past. They may have trouble moving forward and working through their pain because they aren't yet willing to accept that the past is officially over. It's never easy to look at what's been lost, but it's unbearable when the future seems just as painful and uncertain. When the brokenhearted arrive at this point in their journey, they will need our love and support in order to face the unknown with courage and resolve. As we greet them, let us do so with the wisdom of Anne Lamott whispering in our ears, "To offer your beloved people Average and Boring is such grace—no answers, no plans for their damaged lives, no position on their feelings. The best gift to the bereaved is your familiar, boring love; clean sheets and a pillow. Stock up on their favorite yogurt. Welcome their dogs."[9]

7.

"DON'T TRY TO FIX ME; I DON'T NEED YOUR CRITIQUE"

Emotions are complicated because they refuse to be quantified, which is frustrating to those of us who are "fixers." While the bereaved are still in a state of shock and trying to articulate how they feel, the sad truth is that most of us have already stopped listening. It's disconcerting when we assume we understand the depth of someone's pain and create an action plan for them to follow, especially when our assessment of their needs might be completely off base. When we decide what it best for them and try to enforce our agenda, we gradually become emotionally unavailable to the very people we are trying to support. We may even grow frustrated with their suffering and wonder why they are ungrateful or reject our advice. Meanwhile, our loved ones are desperate for our assistance, but feel pressured to receive it in a way they may not want or need. Many are simultaneously appreciative of our willingness to be involved and offended by the way we go about it. They find themselves stuck in the hopeless and unproductive cycle of reaching out for then rejecting the help they are offered. As a result, they feel like their hands are tied because they don't know who is able to provide the level of care they desire.

Several years ago, a friend and I were trying to advocate for a group of people who were seeking help from a counseling program we had been through ourselves. Based on our first-hand experience and the stories we heard from some of the participants, we quickly discovered several common frustrations with the process. Many people joined the program because they were desperately looking for counsel, but they did not feel like they were being heard. They complained about receiving generic feedback and were discouraged because they were not working through their issues or progressing as they had hoped. My friend and I felt similarly during our experience, but were fortunate enough to receive guidance and support through other means. We communicated our concerns to the program directors, but they did not agree with a few key issues we brought to their attention: namely, that people were not getting better, even though they were willing to do the work necessary to get there.

Many are simultaneously appreciative of our willingness to be involved and offended by the way we go about it.

Instead, those with the power to change the curriculum and adapt their program to better serve the participants' needs were not interested in our constructive criticism. Though the staff members meant well, in my opinion, they simply were not qualified to deal with the depth of pain many of the people were experiencing. Rather than developing additional resources or providing educational workshops for their counselors to receive advanced training, they maintained that the participants received proper care. They believed their program worked, and while it was never overtly discussed, they implied that those who were dissatisfied with the program were the ones who were actually at fault because they were refusing to get better.

It's like having a limb torn off and being offered a Band-Aid to stop the bleeding.

Though I affirm the legitimacy of the popular saying, "You can't help someone who doesn't want help," it didn't apply to the people who were disappointed in the program. The people I spoke to were very interested in change. Many of them had experienced significant trauma and were ready to move forward in their lives, but they didn't know how to do it. They were looking for an acute type of care and practical advice, but they didn't get it. In a physical sense, I liken it to having a limb torn off and being offered a Band-Aid to stop the bleeding. Pretend you are the person who lost their limb. You know if you don't find a surgeon, you're going to bleed to death. You also know if you can find the appropriate care, your survival rate drastically increases, even if surviving means learning to live without the limb you wish was still attached. As you fight for your life, a friend hears your cries and offers you a Band-Aid. Your heart sinks, because you know it will not stop the bleeding but your friend remains convinced it's going to help, and becomes increasingly annoyed at your lack of interest. After all, they have had cuts before, and it healed quickly after they covered it with a Band-Aid. Obviously, if you would just do the same thing, you'd be fine too; it's so straightforward.

In the meantime, your friend has grown deaf to your screams because they are focused on getting you to accept their offer. Their preoccupation with getting you to listen to them has blinded them to the blood gushing all around you. All the while, you keep trying to get them to understand that they are not actually helping you. Their method isn't working because your wound is so much deeper than they realize and they've only helped mend surface level cuts before. You're not getting better, but are actually getting worse the more time passes and no legitimate help is extended. However, your pleas are in vain and you keep bleeding. Your friend keeps offering you Band-Aids, and eventually you are forced to walk away from them altogether, out of necessity: If you don't find someone who can treat the severity of your wound, you'll die. Imagine the absurdity of that response and then consider how it is exactly the kind of reaction people in emotional pain experience on a continual basis. It is the unfortunate reality so many of our loved ones feel when we take it upon ourselves to "fix" their emotional pain with a "one size fits all" approach to healing.

It's a lot easier to critique the way someone is handling a situation than it is to have compassion for them.

Another way we inflict wounds is by asking questions people don't have the answers to and then criticizing their decisions. In the wake of a crisis, emotions are high and shock is pervasive. People are just trying to take it and are still in a state of disbelief, wondering how they got where they are. The immediate need is validation and empathy, but too often, our immediate response is judgment. Last I checked, judgment doesn't inspire change. It's like trying to encourage someone to lose weight by calling them "fat" and "lazy." Not only does that hurt their feelings and deflate their self-esteem, but it makes them even less inclined to make healthier choices because they feel too ashamed to start.

It's a lot easier to critique the way someone is handling a situation than it is to have compassion for them. The truth is, none of us know what we would do if we found ourselves in their shoes, anyway. We can make predictions, of course, but if we actually had to live it, all bets are off. It's easy to concoct a plan of action in the hypothetical world, but it's altogether different to live it out in real life. I can't count how many times I've shared a heartache with someone only to have them immediately dismiss what I said and start telling me how I should feel, and what I am or am not allowed to do in response. I've watched the same type of interactions play out repeatedly in the lives of many close friends as well. It's the friend who has been diagnosed with cancer only to discover everyone they know is as doctor. *Well, maybe not a doctor, doctor.* But they certainly think they are just as qualified to offer medical advice. Since they read an article online they are convinced they know every dietary change to implement in addition to the kind of treatments or procedures their friend needs, or needs to avoid. This type of help presents itself in a number of ways, but it's not actually helpful because, even when healthy, no one likes a "know-it-all."

When a person has undergone severe emotional trauma related to abuse, they need to have the freedom to examine what they've been through without additional pressure from us.

Maybe you have a friend whose husband had an affair. Let's call her Judy. Amid the devastation and confusion, people are anxious to "help." Upon hearing of her situation, they offer an influx of advice. "You can't get a divorce. Think of the children," they say. It's an alarmingly popular response.

For starters, maybe Judy never mentioned divorce. Maybe she is still trying to wrap her head around the situation and isn't even ready to think about making a plan for the next chapter of her life. Maybe that won't come until much later. Instead of acknowledging that Judy's heart is breaking as a result of her husband's infidelity, they ignore it and focus on what she has to do to fix it. They don't sit with her or overly concern themselves about her deep feelings of betrayal. They don't listen to her fears about the future. Rather, she's continuously inundated with the reasons why she needs to take a particular course of action, as the responsibility to keep her family together is placed solely on her shoulders. Though many are quick to tell her what she has to do and when she has to do it, few take the time to ask her how she feels about everything that has transpired.

The journey toward wholeness and freedom involves a painful unraveling, but its destination is beauty.

Another deeply disturbing trend among "fixers" is readily seen among those who have been abused. Often, before people express sympathy for the victim, if they ever do at all, they strongly encourage the wounded to forgive and even reconcile with their abusers. Theoretically, I'm in favor of forgiveness, though practically, it's taken a lot of convincing and hard work to implement. Depending on the circumstances, I'm also in favor of reconciliation. However, I'm against pressuring people into doing something they are not ready to do, and I'm especially against trivializing the trauma people have experienced. Unfortunately, that's exactly what we do when we skip the empathizing part and instead rattle off an emotional "to-do list" for how to get over the pain. We stand by, nagging our loved ones to get down to it so we can check each step off the list.

When a person has undergone severe emotional trauma related to abuse, they need to have the freedom to examine what they've been through without additional pressure from us. They need permission to feel their feelings. They need us to be the Robin Williams to their Matt Damon and continually tell them "it's not [their] fault."[1] They need us to encourage them to be compassionate towards themselves, not impatient with their struggles. They need to know the journey toward wholeness and freedom involves a painful unraveling, but its destination is beauty.

If we place unnecessary and unrealistic expectations on someone who is hurting, it piles on the guilt. The guilt is even more severe for those who honestly wish they were further along but, for any number of reasons, aren't there yet. When people feel ashamed about their lack of progress, it's tempting to pretend they've done the necessary work of healing in order to avoid further judgment and criticism. Jon Acuff says, "The problem is not our feelings. The problem is that we have feelings about our feelings."[2] With that in mind, we can conclude that a person in emotional pain is likely experiencing some degree of negative self-talk about how they *should* be feeling. Yet, the insensitivity of our culture combined with the desire to downplay what they are going through can make the grieving feel badly about how they are processing their pain. It doesn't help when we directly or indirectly add fuel to the fire. We have a tendency to compare ourselves and others in just about every conceivable manner. Despite knowing the comparison game usually leads nowhere good, we find it too irresistible to opt out. Consequently, many people in pain silently judge and shame themselves for the things they think they should be doing, but aren't.

In an attempt to show our friend how much we understand their pain, we turn into a tragic one-upper.

Then we "help" them by suggesting things they should do not realizing the pressure we put on our friends who are learning to cope with their loss. Our desire to protect, combined with the fear of vulnerability, distorts our perspective and motivates us to find a way to remedy the pain. We talk about people we know who've experienced suffering and how well they handled everything. We suggest they do what our other friend did, so that they can get back to normal quickly. Or in an attempt to show our friend how much we understand their pain, we turn into a tragic one-upper. Whether it's our own experience or someone else's story, we start to describe how much worse someone else's situation is compared to theirs. It's unpleasant to be on the receiving end of that conversation. What is the expected outcome anyway? That the person we love will feel their pain is negated because it's not as bad as that of others? That they will have to console us or focus their energy on someone else's problems? There aren't many positive outcomes. Granted, there are times when someone is so immersed in their own pain that they need to be reminded that other people suffer too in order to gain a healthier perspective. However, we do not want the bereaved to think something is wrong with them because, comparatively, other people have been through worse and coped much better. If we make the brokenhearted feel guilty that their hearts are actually broken, they may start to hide the truth, even from themselves. Suppressing their emotions only works for so long before it starts leaking out in other places—and if our attitudes encourage a habit of hiding, it will only delay their healing.

The good news is all of this is completely avoidable. I've discovered an interesting paradox: If we become the type of person who does not force our opinion on others, we actually become the type of person people ask for advice. Wisdom is incredibly valuable and practical. If we have the ability to provide insight and advice in a painful situation, it is a gift. If we are sensitive about how we use our gift, we will be surprised by how many people are interested in listening to what we have to say.

I've discovered an interesting paradox: If we become the type of person who does not force our opinion on others, we actually become the type of person people ask for advice.

Before we have the opportunity to speak into someone's life, however, it must be clear that we value the relational bond Relationships rise and fall on the virtues of trust and respect, so if we are sincere and empathetic, the advice we offer will be a natural overflow of who we are and the relational connection we've already established. When we desire understanding, we are far more willing to listen before we speak and far less likely to overstep boundaries. Being willing to wait and hope without knowing all the answers is an uncommon and admirable trait; the people in our life will take notice and seek us out because of it. Then, when they are open to advice, they will initiate the conversation.

When I am uncertain about what to say or how to be a good friend to someone, I remind myself of the basics: "One who loves a pure heart and who speaks with grace will have the king for a friend."[3] Sometimes we make things so much more complicated than they need to be. We think we have to know what to do at every moment, but all we really need to do is to be a sincere friend, to genuinely love the people in our lives. We all need a friend whose words are honest and graceful, whose commitment to us is unwavering, and each one of us can become that kind of friend as we continue to practice these simple truths.

8.
"JUST BE STRONG"

Most of us have a narrow-minded understanding of strength. We define it primarily on the observable, external characteristics and strive to fit the ideal. The physical strength of an individual is accepted as legitimate because it is easily identifiable to the naked eye. We can know the kind of strength a person is capable of when they are put to the test because we can quantify the results. It's very straightforward.

In our day and age, "strength" has become synonymous with "self-sufficient" and any signs of dependence are met with disdain. Strength is about being the best and achieving impressive feats. It's a way to show how capable we are without saying a word, a way to intimidate our competition to back down without a fight.

However, if we only focus our attention on the external, we will miss out on many interesting things going on under the surface. Though the interior world of a person is private and largely unseen, we're able to see the characteristics of inner strength manifest themselves in tangible ways if we pay attention long enough.

A while back, I started reading about various Olympians and other high-level performers. I'm a musician and, though it's a very different kind of work, I was curious what I would discover about people who've been successful in very competitive fields. I was interested in finding out what things made them rise to the top and if those things were similar across the board. The more I read, the more I could predict what they would say in advance.

In our day and age, "strength" has become synonymous with "self-sufficient" and any signs of dependence are met with disdain.

Even among people competing at the highest level physically, the distinguishing factor in their success was their ability to be mentally tough. Admittedly, physical toughness was a prerequisite. However, the physical preparation was apparent to the competitors; they expected to make sacrifices to train their bodies. Though they are guided by coaches and dietitians in order to push their bodies to the limit and maximize their results, at a certain level, the physical differences between the peak performers is minimal. For most of these individuals, only a few seconds separates the first from the last, and that's an extremely narrow margin.

Psychologists step in to help competitors manage the pressure of that narrow margin. When everyone competing is already doing all they can do to prepare physically, the only way to gain an advantage is through mental preparation. Those individuals who are able to focus and remain calm, perform the best under pressure. In a high intensity environment, it's easy to be thrown off kilter by a surge of emotions, which is why the strongest competitors practice their mental game. They use visualization techniques and develop rituals to help themselves prepare. Then, when the stakes are high, they are able to remain calm because they have the mental stamina necessary to combat the fearful thoughts fighting for control. In his book *Zero Regrets*, eight-time Olympic medalist Apolo Ohno writes, "Fear kills your potential to be who you are and who you can become. The trick is to acknowledge it—and then let it go."[1]

The most successful people value inner strength and work to develop their "fear management" system. Everyone, regardless of how well put together they may appear, has cracks in their armor. Those who have the courage to acknowledge their fears have the advantage, because they can identify where they need help. They know their vulnerabilities are not their real enemy and are willing to confront them head on.

To the casual observer, this type of strength may not look very strong at all. In fact, it might even look like the exact opposite. However, we do ourselves a disservice when we believe that displaying emotion is a sign of weakness because it is far from the truth. We have this misconception that strength and weakness are at odds with each other.

That we have the choice to be either strong or weak, one or the other. This is not a true reflection of reality. It is more accurate to view them along a spectrum. Both strength and weakness live inside each person, though they may present themselves in different ways and different times. If we are strong, we may be weak in the future. If we are weak, we are not hopelessly so.

I've heard stories about brave WWII soldiers who cried before battle, because they chose to face their fears. They were willing to look at circumstances that evoked deep fear within them and allowed themselves to experience a very appropriate emotional response. As a result, many of those men demonstrated immense courage in a time of great danger and became heroic warriors on the field. Yet, their courage did not originate in the midst of battle; it started taking root long before they even set foot on the ground. The valiant soldiers were able to pass their test when the stakes were high because they had developed a habit of saying, "yes," even when they were afraid. They did not pretend they were invincible, but understood their own mortality and decided to press on regardless. Though they experienced the weight of that decision emotionally, only a fool would call them weak.

As the Olympic athletes and brave soldiers demonstrate, it does not serve us well to pretend we are fearless and strong one hundred percent of the time. It's simply not a reality and it's exhausting. Equally upsetting is the belief that an honest display of emotion is synonymous with weakness. If we truly want the brokenhearted to grieve and heal, we have to give them permission to look at the hard things and react emotionally. We can't expect them to tell us how they feel and look to us for support if we try to shut down every inkling of sorrow they express. Our loved ones need to know we can take it. They need to know the whole world won't fall apart even if they do. They need us to reassure them that we won't run away, even though we're afraid too.

We can't expect people to tell us how they feel and look to us for support if we try to shut down every inkling of sorrow they express.

One of the greatest gifts we can give someone is to let them know we are strong enough to hold their strength if they need to lay it down for a while. When we understand this, we can be more compassionate towards those we love when, in a season of loss, they aren't as strong as they used to be. Since strength is an attribute not an identity, we have the capacity to grow and become stronger. Therefore, a deficit of strength is not a moral failing either. When we've used all the strength we've stored up, we simply need to be replenished. Isaiah 40:30-31 speaks to this principle: "Even youths grow tired and weary, and young men stumble and fall; but those who hope in the Lord will renew their strength. They will soar on wings like eagles, they will run and not grow weary, they will walk and not be faint."[2]

As indicated in the verse above, I believe we receive a renewed sense of strength from God. He is the source of our strength and the only one whose strength is not rationed out but always in abundance. However, I also believe God gave us each other for a reason and there is strength in numbers. People in pain need to know they can draw on the strength of their community when they're depleted. When life requires more than we have to give, it's comforting to know that we can become stronger, simply by allowing the strength of God and our friends to wash over us. As Donald Miller writes in his book, *Blue Like Jazz*, "Strength, inner strength comes from receiving love as much as it comes from giving it. The prayer I pray for all my friends is that they will be able to receive love."[3]

Scripture teaches us a valuable lesson about borrowing some of our strength from community. Community is an immense blessing; it allows us to share the load with other people and take turns supporting the friend in crisis. It also provides an outlet for both the grief-stricken and the caregivers to receive support and recharge, so they don't burn out. There is a story in the Bible that illustrates this concept well. Moses was tasked with leading the Israelites out of Egypt, and for those familiar with the story, it was a long journey. At one point, they were attacked by the Amalekite army. Moses went to the top of a hill overlooking the battle and brought his staff, through which God did many powerful acts, along with him. When Moses lifted up his staff, the Israelite army would prevail. But when he lowered it, the Amalekites would overpower them.

Since strength is an attribute not an identity, we have the capacity to grow and become stronger.

Eventually, Moses grew tired and needed to rely on help from his community to accomplish his task. His brother Aaron and a man named Hur gave him a rock to sit on. Then the men stood on each side of Moses and held up his hands until sunrise and the Israelites were victorious.[4] Isn't it interesting that Moses friends' held up his hands *until sunrise*? In other words, as the men surrounded Moses and held up his hands, it was dark outside. Yet, they remained with him in the darkness; they supported him until the light of the sun ushered in a new day, and a triumphant one at that. It's a beautiful picture of the power of community, and it's a great point of reference for those of us who want to help our friends but don't know where to begin.

When the grief is too much for our loved ones to bear alone, as their supporters, it's our time to shine. We are there to hold up their arms, to provide the necessary backup so they can keep fighting another day. We are there to infuse them with the strength of an entire community and give them the confidence to keep going when they'd rather give up. We're there to remind them if they drop the ball, we'll chase it down and hold onto it, until they're ready to pick it up again.

They remained with him in the darkness; they supported him until the light of the sun ushered in a new day.

Strength often accomplishes its best work in subtle ways, content to play a supporting role. It can be elusive and surprise us when it shows up in humility and a quiet confidence. In the midst of grief, our loving care plants a seed of strength inside the brokenhearted. When we patiently attend to the bereaved, it is like daily water that encourages the seed to take root and grow, though, at times, it may spill back out in the form of tears. As we faithfully tend to the grieving, we anticipate the warmth of the sun, and trust that, eventually, the little seed will give birth to new life.

9.
"LET ME BE WEAK"

If we learn to see strength and weakness on a continuum, we will start to come to terms with the weaknesses that live inside of us. Hopefully, this new awareness will lead us to an attitude of compassion toward our shortcomings instead of self-contempt and shame, and we will become more understanding when we see the people in our lives struggling, because we will understand it as simply part of the human experience.

But if you find yourself feeling resistant when people around you are vulnerable and sharing uncomfortable truths, in all likelihood, the root of the problem resides in you and not the person sharing. If you don't care for this type of authenticity in your relationships, you probably don't permit it in yourself either. And here's the real trick: if you really want to help the people around you cope with their experiences, you also have to be willing to do the work on yourself.

A few years ago, I was sitting on the couch in my counselor's office telling her everything I was afraid of and how I didn't like being weak. I was shocked when she called me out on a few things.

"So let me get this straight. If you're afraid of something that means you're weak?"

"Exactly," I said.

"Just because you feel afraid as you confront a person or issue, does not mean you are weak. I have another word for that: courage."[1]

Just because you feel afraid as you confront a person or issue, does not mean you are weak. I have another word for that: courage.

Often, what we define as weakness in ourselves could more accurately be described as courage. We spend an excessive amount of energy trying to hide the parts of ourselves we're embarrassed we even have. Since everyone knows what it's like to be afraid at one point or another, theoretically, we shouldn't have any problem talking about our fears or relating to others when they share theirs. However, shame likes to attach itself to fear. Consequently, when we feel afraid, we often succumb to shame's mandate of secrecy, instead of sharing our concerns with our inner circle.

Alternatively, those who are courageous enough to share their struggles and ask for help often discover an interesting phenomenon; they get it. Admitting fear proves challenging in and of itself, but when we realize we need communal support and have to actually ask for help, it can feel unbearable. We are much more comfortable being the person extending help to someone else than we are asking for it for ourselves. As long as things are going well in our lives and we feel in control, it's easy to maintain this attitude of self-sufficiency. However, the strict standards of independence we adhere to are not as harmless as we envision them to be when these imbalanced ideals creep into our subconscious thoughts and influence us in ways we might not notice. According to Brené Brown, "When [we] cannot ask for and accept help without [self] judgment, then we cannot offer help without judgment either."[2] Let that sink in for a minute. If we refuse to confess our personal weaknesses, then we will secretly judge others for theirs. Conversely, if we are willing to offend our sense of pride, embrace the discomfort of vulnerability, and talk about our worries, not only will we become healthier people ourselves but we will also develop a secret power to help others in pain.

Many of us are afflicted with unnecessary shame because we are not as invincible as we'd like to think we are and have convinced ourselves that everyone else is perfect. When we are willing to acknowledge our own fears and insecurities, we are finally able to be a nonthreatening confidant to someone who is struggling. To a person in emotional turmoil, there is immense healing available in two little words: "Me too." It's like a healing balm for the heart.

If you find yourself feeling resistant when people around you are vulnerable and sharing uncomfortable truths, in all likelihood, the root of the problem resides in you and not the person sharing.

Vulnerability increases trust and establishes credibility within our relationships. It also deepens empathy, which, by default, deepens our level of connectedness. While I do not advise "airing our dirty laundry" to just anyone, I am a major proponent of being transparent with a trusted few. When we are tasked with loving the people in our lives as they work through their grief, it is paramount that we listen and receive the things they want to share with us. As Brené Brown suggests, "Vulnerability is the last thing [we] want [others] to see in [us], but the first thing [we] look for in [others]."[3] The more life we live, the more we'll realize the gift of honest friendship and the less we'll try to impress others by pretending we always have our act together. We'll be free to need each other without self-imposed condemnation and divulge the times we only "get by with a little help from [our] friends."[4]

While we fear our shortcomings will disqualify us from being loved and accepted, the comforting reality is that we usually identify with each other's weaknesses more than their strengths. Consider the following example, based in part on a true story. Two accomplished presenters were invited to speak on similar topics at the same conference, but the way the audience reacted to each presenter was drastically different. The first speaker opened with a clip of his professional accomplishments, but was poorly received. To the listeners, he came across as pretentious. In reality, he's not the jerk people at the conference perceive him to be. He had many obstacles throughout his journey to the top but chose not to share them, and his silence spoke volumes. Many factors could have influenced his decision. Maybe he was too afraid to share them publically. Or perhaps he thought the audience only wanted to hear about the good decisions he made, as if sharing the mistakes he made along the way would ruin his credibility. Regardless, because he chose to remain silent, he failed to establish a connection with his audience. More than that, he actually repelled them.

To a person in emotional turmoil, there is immense healing available in two little words: "Me too."

Contrast the first presenter's approach with the second, and we'll discover a drastically different result. The second presenter introduced himself and shared failure after failure. He spoke about the years of struggle, the self-doubt, the agony of being misunderstood, and the constant wondering if he would ever overcome the challenges in front of him. He also talked about a few "lucky breaks" and the numerous individuals who helped him along the way. When he finally shared about his many successes, the audience was incredibly moved. They were able to see themselves in the speaker and were hopeful about their own futures. They related to the ups and downs and sometimes circular pathways he traveled on the road to success. By the time he ended his presentation, the audience was emotionally involved. They identify with and celebrate his story, not just the end result.

The vulnerability of the second presenter distinguished him from everyone else at the conference. While one presenter repulsed the people he was trying to reach, the other inspired them to action, all because he was willing to share his shortcomings. His story resonated with people because it was real, more than it was pretty. Likewise, if we can encourage our grieving friends to value the complete version of their story more than the polished one, we will start to see strength rise up inside of them.

The moment someone is willing to own their weakness is the exact moment they start to become stronger. This concept holds true in the physical realm as well as the spiritual. Jim Cymbala notes this phenomenon when he writes, "I discovered an astonishing truth: God is attracted to weakness. He can't resist those who humbly and honestly admit how desperately they need him."[5] I find it disheartening that so many people think they have to be perfect in order for God to love them or, at least, for God to help them. Christianity teaches that Jesus was perfect for us, so we don't have to be. Because we believe He offered Himself as sacrifice on our behalf, not only are we forgiven, but we are also free to be honest with God without fear of being rejected. Thankfully, as Dave Ohlerking points out, "honesty acknowledges both weakness and strength."[6]

To be completely honest, I'd rather God just take away my pain instead of giving me the grace to endure it.

The Bible speaks of God's strength being made perfect in our weakness. The Apostle Paul, who is responsible for writing most of the New Testament, wrote about a tormenting "thorn in his flesh."[7] Three times, he pleaded with God to take it away, but God did not remove the thorn. Instead, He poured His grace into Paul, in the form of supernatural strength, so that he could not only endure the pain but also keep ministering to—well—just about everyone. Paul goes on to say that he "will boast all the more gladly in his weakness," so that "the power of Christ may rest on [him]."[8]

To be completely honest, I'd rather God just take away my pain instead of giving me the grace to endure it. I'm not particularly interested in bragging about my weakness either. If you're anything like me, I'm sure you can relate. For reasons I cannot fully explain, living in this broken world, means we will inevitably face tragedies we cannot undo. We are not exempt from hardship or heartbreak, and as we try to comfort the people we love as they struggle to cope with immense loss, may we also find comfort in knowing there is unlikely power in weakness.

Contrary to popular thought, we're often given more than we can handle. However, God does not expect us to muster up the strength and bear it alone. Instead, as we cry out for the grace to endure loss and care for those who are hurting, our cries for help are met with understanding and involvement. Over and over again, we see examples of God extending his kindness and power toward those who are at the end of their rope. As Alan Scot says, "In the kingdom of God, compassion is the currency of authority"; the weak are accepted and favored to receive as much strength as they need.[9]

Just to make sure we understand the depth of His love for us, especially in our worst moments, God reveals His character to us throughout the pages of Scripture. In the Psalms, He lifts us out of the pit of destruction.[10] In Hosea, He's the doorway of hope in our time of trouble.[11] In Luke, He's the Father who shamelessly runs to welcome the son who made a mess of his life.[12] In Matthew, He's the light that breaks forth into darkness and brings hope to those living in the shadow of death.[13] He's always doing the unthinkable and unexpected. Instead of judging us when we are so hurt and disappointed that we start to walk away from our faith, He walks away with us until we are able to believe again.[14] He embraces the weak, the rejected, and the people who have no hope of dealing with their problems on their own. He moves directly towards the people everyone else runs away from, including the grief-stricken, enveloped in their pain.

The reality is that God has never been overly concerned with our strength, or our weakness, for that matter.

Consider the scandalous people Jesus selected as His disciples. He didn't choose the most qualified or socially impressive; he picked the ordinary men. He even picked the rejects. He had every opportunity to make his team into a powerhouse of the most skilled and accomplished, but instead, as my former pastor likes to say, "He chose the 'JV' team."[15] The reality is that God has never been overly concerned with our strength, or our weakness, for that matter. In fact, Psalm 147:10 reveals, "His pleasure is not in the strength of the horse, nor His delight in the legs of the warrior; the LORD delights in those who fear [reverence] Him, who put their hope in His unfailing love."[16] As long as we're connected to Him, we don't have to be too concerned about out weakness either. Since He is strong enough for us all, we can fill up our "strength tank" as often as we'd like and simply receive our sustenance.

In a similar manner, when we are not intimidated by the depth of a person's need and embrace the vulnerable in our midst, the potential for understanding and healing increases dramatically. When we emulate the character of God through our love and support for our friends in pain, they will know they can safely tell us anything. We will be a source of comfort to them because we will not try to silence them when they want to speak or force a conversation when they need to be still. They will feel the sense of security they are longing for, and we will champion their courageous vulnerability. For our loved ones to know we are strong enough to let them be weak is an incredible gift. To sit with them and their pain without expectation or demands about how they must become stronger is a blessing of true friendship.

10.

"WHEN THERE'S NOTHING LEFT TO DO, YOU'LL HAVE TO PRAY ME THROUGH"

On a good day, prayer is a taboo subject. We don't know how to feel about it because we can't quite figure out how it works or if it works, for that matter. Those of you, who, like myself, are familiar with the tenets of the Christian faith, might be able to give a decent, theological explanation about what happens when we pray. Though I could also do that, it doesn't make prayer any less mysterious to me. Sometimes, we pray and get exactly what we ask for; other times, we pray and it seems like nothing happens. Then, there are the times when we don't pray at all, and everything still works out exactly as planned. It's perplexing, to say the least. If you have not experienced it firsthand, most of you have at least heard a few miraculous stories about the power of prayer in other people's lives. Depending on your personal beliefs, those stories will either inspire or confuse you, or perhaps make you even more skeptical. Regardless, prayer is often a topic of conversation in times of crisis, and, as such, is worth exploring a little more in depth.

Sometimes, we have a very transactional approach to prayer and try to turn it into an easy-to-follow formula, designed to achieve maximum results. Though the Bible is filled with practical insights about prayer, most famously from Jesus in what we commonly refer to as "The Lord's Prayer," I don't believe we're supposed to use it as a getting what we want. When we approach God as though He were a genie and thus, obligated to, at least, give us the top three wishes we ask for, we might be disappointed with the outcome. Conversely, many people are convinced God will only listen to the most urgent requests, and forgo praying altogether, except in emergencies. They don't want to waste time asking for trivial things, in case they need to ask for help for something really important down the road. When the stakes are high and nothing else has worked, it's a last resort; they hope that God will answer their request favorably, since they don't usually bother him.

Sometimes, we pray and get exactly what we ask for; other times, we pray and it seems like nothing happens. Then, there are the times when we don't pray at all, and everything still works out exactly as planned. It's perplexing, to say the least.

Though many people are uncertain about prayer, a lot of people are willing to re-examine it when they're in a desperate situation. Sometimes, we only pray because we have run out of other options. We're not sure what to do, but we figure sending up a few prayers will help us get on God's good side, so He'll be more inclined to help us out. However, prayer is not a means through which we manipulate God; it is an invitation to commune with Him. What if prayer is more relational than transactional? What if it's more like an ongoing conversation than a ceremonial act?

I think the heart of prayer is about trust because it's the foundation of every relationship. Since we're not going to be interested in praying to a God we don't trust, He invites us to get to know Him. Psalm 37:23 tells us, "He delights in every detail of [our] lives," so we don't have to worry He will be uninterested about what we have to say or indifferent toward our needs.[1] In the same way that we bond with our friends and family by spending time together, spending time with God in prayer establishes a bond between us. As the relational bond increases, our sense of security will be rooted in Him, instead of our circumstances. We will start to believe God is not only listening to our prayers but also that He is well able to hold us together when everything else comes unglued. We will grow to trust in the character of God, and develop the kind of confidence described in Isaiah 33:6, believing "he will be the stability of [our] times."[2]

What if prayer is more relational than transactional?

Despite the opportunity to pray about every concern we have, many of us still do not accept the invitation to do so. Prayer is helplessness acknowledged, and it makes me wonder if that is one of the reasons why so many people struggle to pray. Who enjoys the feeling of helplessness? Who likes admitting they need help and can't properly take care of themselves? If we have an aversion to weakness, it's a challenge just to admit it to ourselves. If we're not careful, our insecurities will prevent us from praying because they make us uncomfortable, and we don't like thinking about them.

Prayer can also ignite a sense of panic because it asks our fragile hearts to believe again without guaranteeing things will work out the way we hope. When we're terrified our hearts will be broken and our dreams will be shattered, we struggle to invest emotionally. We don't even want to hope because we are terrified we won't be able to survive another let down if that's the way it unfolds. In times of grief, anger and bitterness can become another obstacle to prayer. Some things are so traumatic, some wounds are so severe, we are simply not interested in talking to God anymore. We may be consumed with feelings of betrayal toward the One who could have prevented our heartbreak but did not.

Prayer is incredibly powerful, but we should not tell someone we will pray for them if we don't mean it; it's not meant to be an excuse for inaction.

If you are a person of prayer and you are concerned about a friend who has experienced a great loss, know that your prayers for them are invaluable, but don't be alarmed if they do not share your enthusiasm. In the aftermath of a tragedy, the wreckage is insurmountable. People who survive traumatic events, become different people as a result of their experiences, and it might take them a while to discover who that new person is and what that new person believes. Be patient with them as they search for the answer, and let their tears be liquid prayers if they cannot formulate words.

It's also worth noting that many people who welcome our prayers, as they suffer through seasons of loss, may be a skeptical about our sincerity. Before we have time to process the information a person has shared with us, we're quick to tell someone we are praying for them. While this is great if it is a true commitment, I fear that, in some cultures, it's become an auto-response to crisis. Occasionally, we use this phrase as a way to lessen our sense of responsibility to care for the suffering in our midst; it's a way to feel involved without actually doing anything.

Prayer is incredibly powerful, but we should not tell someone we will pray for them if we don't mean it; it's not meant to be an excuse for inaction.

Sometimes, we plead for God to intervene when He's already given us the necessary resources to meet the need ourselves, and it's simply a matter of being willing to get involved on a deeper level.

I've also discovered that God may ask us to help answer our own prayers. When someone in pain tells us they have a need, and we ask God to meet their needs, He may choose to do it through us. So often, we forget that the Church is called the body of Christ. If we are His representatives, we should reach out to help in practical and spiritual ways when we have the ability to do so. Sometimes, we plead for God to intervene when He's already given us the necessary resources to meet the need ourselves, and it's simply a matter of being willing to get involved on a deeper level. However, there will likely come a time, when all the practical needs are met, but our friends are still suffering. When we've done everything we can do, but it's not enough, we can still pray.

Our prayers are agents of change—through them, we invite the power of God into our situations and our lives. If we are secure in knowing God welcomes the weak, the brokenhearted, even the skeptical, prayer can become a conduit of strength, healing, and power. Tim Keller reassures us, "What is important is not the number of people praying but the nature of the praying."[3] We can show up with our honest hurts and hopes, disappointments, and confusion and be confident that God will meet us in it. We can, in turn, use the comfort and strength we receive to comfort the hurting in our midst.

So often, things start happening under the surface before they ever manifest in tangible ways. Sometimes, we ask God for things and He gives us a seed. If we nurture the seed, it will eventually sprout new life. The potential for change and an immeasurable influence is contained within a tiny seed, and planted right into the darkness of the dirty soil. That's how I've experienced the power of prayer most often in my own life. Occasionally, I've seen dramatic breakthroughs and immediate change. But often, change has sprouted out of the continual nurturing of the seed. We don't always know what the seed is going to turn into or how it's going to look once it's fully matured, but we know it's alive and things are happening under the surface that will one day appear above ground. When we change our attitude about prayer from something we do when we're all out of options to something we do because it changes things, we'll be more excited to pray and will desire to pray with increasing frequency. We won't feel helpless because we will understand the power that is available to us through prayer.

Perhaps nothing has inspired my prayer life more than the following excerpt from Walter Wink's book, *The Powers That Be: Theology for a New Millennium:*

Our prayers are agents of change—through them, we invite the power of God into our situations and our lives.

"Intercessory prayer is spiritual defiance of what is in the way of what God has promised. Intercession visualizes an alternative future to the one apparently fated by the momentum of current forces. Prayer infuses the air of a time yet to be into the suffocating atmosphere of the present. *History belongs to the intercessors who believe the future into being...*A space opens in the praying person, permitting God to act without violating human freedom. The change in one person thus changes what God can thereby do in that world."[4]

When we are willing to believe for those who have lost their way or are too tired to hope, we usher in the power of God. We become conduits of hope and advocates of grace for our friends. We welcome change in ourselves, so that God can use us to change the world; and we invite Him to start by using us to change the lives of people who mean the world to us.

11.
"GIVE ME TIME; I NEED TO HEAL"

The healing process can feel like an arduous uphill climb, with a vague idea of where the summit is. Many of our grief-stricken friends are so consumed with their pain, they struggle to see beyond it. While we must give them space to experience these emotions, we can also reassure them when they feel like they'll never be happy again. The passing of time will not heal their wounds, as many promise, but it will not drown out all future joy either.

When those suffering are upset about the slow ascent up healing hill, we can help them find beauty in little things: the comfort of a hot cup of coffee on a cold day, the smell of fresh laundry hanging out to dry, the resilience of a flower blossoming in the spring after a rough winter. We can celebrate small victories such as a full day without tears or a genuine laugh about something silly. We can remind them, though the journey is long, they don't have to know the exact route to take as long as they're paying attention to the little light illuminating their next step. C.S. Lewis, reminds us that "day by day nothing changes, but when [we] look back, everything is different."[1] When the monotony of their daily climb seems unbearable as it unfolds in real time, we can encourage our loved ones to persist.

Grief has both a cognitive and emotional component, but we often fail to recognize its complexity. Though hurting people may have an intellectual understanding of their condition and may have even reached a level of acceptance, they could still be suffering acute emotional pain. When we want to help but cannot see the multiple dimensions of healing, we can only help people progress so far. Much of this book has been about shedding light on the emotional component of grief and its many obstacles, for that very reason. Though many of our dearest friends may be mentally stable and at peace, their emotions are likely creating an internal ruckus. Emotional turmoil, though ruthless and overwhelming by nature, is to be expected after a loss. If we could spare our loved ones the excruciating pain of working through it, we undoubtedly would. However, the gradual, yet imperceptible, emotional work is a necessary part of the healing process. The unfortunate reality is that healing, like time, does its own thing. No matter how much we wish it to speed up, it keeps a steady pace and refuses to be manipulated.

The passing of time will not heal their wounds, as many promise, but it will not drown out all future joy either.

Sometimes, the most seemingly futile things are the most fundamental part of healing. A few months ago, I felt stuck in a cycle of emotional frustration and professional setbacks. I was driving home from my weekly pottery class, half-praying, half-complaining about my predicament. I was discouraged by the lack of results I saw from my hard work and wondered whether it was all in vain. I felt like I was just spinning around in circles, doing the same things over and over again, not progressing. As I got off the exit and turned onto my street, an image suddenly popped into my head; I saw a lump of clay, spinning around on a wheel-head. Just like that, a singular mental picture refocused my attention and breathed new life into my weary soul.

The gradual, yet imperceptible, emotional work is a necessary part of the healing process.

They say life imitates art. Or maybe, art imitates life. From the time I've spent working with clay, I've learned the connection between the two is particularly strong. Throughout my life, I've spent countless hours in many different pottery studios. These days, I'm more of a hobbyist and primarily create things for fun, but I've definitely put in my time. Based on the many profound lessons I've learned about life, and the amount of fun I've had creating, I'm convinced it's been time well spent.

Being a potter has given me an appreciation for the various properties and processes clay must go through from conception to finished product. The image that came to mind as I was driving was about a process called "centering." It is one of the first techniques a potter learns because it is a foundational part of wheel-throwing. With practice, you can learn to master this step, but you will never graduate from it. Every single piece of clay, regardless of what it will become, must first be centered before it can be formed into the desired shape.

With practice, you can learn to master this step, but you will never graduate from it.

Interestingly enough, when a potter centers a piece of clay, the clay spins around on the wheel in continuous circles. What looks like aimlessness, will after several revolutions, become a solid foundation, as the clay succumbs to centrifugal force and the pressure of the potter's hand. The potter applies pressure to strategic places and, inch by inch, the clay moves towards the center. After it is completely centered, and only after it is completely centered, the potter is able to start shaping the clay into the desired end product. What appears to be unproductive is, in actuality the birthplace of change. Likewise, when it appears as though nothing is happening, our grieving friends may gradually be finding their way back to center. It might appear as though their progress is stunted, but our patience with them will prove to be an invaluable gift. After all, change happens internally first and it isn't always easy to recognize.

A potter also knows that timing is of utmost importance. Because the consistency of the clay will fluctuate between different stages of wetness and dryness, certain parts of the process must be done at a specific time. A good potter will know which stage their pieces are in, how long they need to remain a particular consistency, and what can or cannot be accomplished at that time. Like the clay, our loved ones are being guided by the Master's hand, though it is not always apparent. Even though the process is messy and looks a lot like walking in circles, they are not spinning around in vain—they are becoming.

Even though the process is messy and looks a lot like walking in circles, they are not spinning around in vain — they are becoming.

Our friends will naturally move through various stages of grief. As with clay, certain parts of their healing process will require them to remain in a particular stage in order to complete the work necessary to move on to the next stage. As caregivers and friends, we need to do our best to protect their process and allow them to stay in a particular stage if they still have work to do there; we don't need to pressure them to move in a direction that will throw them off course. If a potter desires to keep the clay a specific consistency, in order to complete the work that must be accomplished in that stage, they will often manipulate the environmental surroundings. For example, if they wanted their clay to retain its moisture, they might spritz it with water or wrap it in a plastic bag. In a similar manner, if we notice our loved one is trying to move through their grief prematurely, we can intervene. While I'm not suggesting we try to manipulate anyone, I believe the way we interact with the bereaved, powerfully influences the choices they make. Like a plastic bag covers the clay and protects it from drying out too quickly, we help shield the suffering from unhealthy external influences, by surrounding them with our love and patience.

If we trust the healing process and nurture our people as they grow incrementally, they'll be more likely to follow our lead and cut themselves a break. In time, they'll learn to "trust the winter seasons [of life],...when nothing moves perceptively and [they] think [they] are just standing stagnant."[2] They'll discover that the Potter knows how to reclaim broken lives and form them into new vessels. Then, one day, we will be privileged to watch as our loved ones emerge with newfound strength, beauty, and purpose.

12.

"I DON'T WANT TO HIDE THE WAY I FEEL"

Adversity and loss have a way of calling out our inner soldiers and challenging us to fight for ourselves and our loved ones. They can be so relentless that we almost succumb under pressure. However, when we persist and rise up to fight another day, we choose hope, and it changes our psychology. In his book, *David and Goliath*, Malcolm Gladwell tells a story about a Nazi attack on London.[1] (Throughout the story, He references J.T. MacCurdy's book, *The Structure of Morale*, which examines the psychological effect of war on civilians.) The Nazi's were trying to intimidate the Brits and destroy their morale before they even had a chance to fight, but an interesting thing happened. While they bombed the towns, the public had three distinct responses based on their proximity to the explosions: the direct hit, the near miss, and the distant miss. Obviously, not everyone survived, and those who were *hit directly* died. While tragic, the percentage of the population who were hit directly and died, were not around to spread fear or panic throughout the community. Those in the *near miss* group, who were injured but lived, had the hardest time after the attack. They experienced the trauma

125

firsthand and lived to tell about it. Many in this group struggled to overcome fear; their recovery was the hardest. The members of the *distant miss* group, who heard the bombings but escaped unharmed, as well as those in the *near miss* group who were able to work through their pain, developed a new and contagious confidence.[2]

Adversity and loss have a way of calling out our inner soldiers and challenging us to fight for ourselves and our loved ones.

It turns out there is truth to the old saying, "what doesn't kill you makes you stronger." Though the Germans had hoped to deflate British morale with their attacks, the opposite proved true. Since the majority of the survivors experienced *distant misses,* and felt invincible because they beat the odds, the attacks actually served to strengthen their resolve. Though the Londoners were initially afraid and felt impending doom, when they escaped without harm, it changed their mentality. MacCurdy discovered, "We are all of us not merely liable to fear, we are also prone to be afraid of being afraid, and the conquering of fear produces exhilaration…The contrast between the previous apprehension and the present relief and feeling of security promotes a self-confidence that is the very father and mother of courage."[3] So it is in our lives as well: when the bombs around us go off and threaten to take us out, but we survive, we become courageous. We may even become courageous enough to embrace vulnerability.

When we persist and rise up to fight another day, we choose hope, and it changes our psychology.

We're all looking for love and acceptance. Though we struggle to share the embarrassing and painful parts of our lives, it is only by being willing to let our guard down that we will be able to let anyone else in. As we grow in our understanding of what authentic connection looks like, we will also notice growth in our level of empathy, trust, and overall relational satisfaction.

When we become more comfortable with the uncomfortable, we will notice a greater depth in ourselves and value these characteristics in others, instead of rushing to judgment. With this newfound marriage of compassion and boldness, we will be more apt to simply show up as we are, flaws and all. We'll agree with Thomas Merton's wise observation, "The beginning of love is to let those we love be perfectly themselves, and not to twist them to fit our own image. Otherwise, we love only the reflection of ourselves we find in them."[4]

We, the caregivers, supporters, hand-holders, hug-givers, and friends of those experiencing loss, have a critical role to play. We are going to be the first responders when tragedy strikes their world. We are the ones they will look to when they don't know what to do. Allowing them to be "perfectly themselves," even in their darkest moments, is the most loving thing we can offer them. Though I wish none of us would ever have to live those moments in the first place, I know it is an unlikely reality. At some point, we will all take a turn being the one in pain and the one comforting those in pain; we'll become acquainted with both sides eventually. Though bittersweet, the very fact that we will all have rough moments in life prepares us for being the kind of friend a grieving person would welcome in their time of need. When we live through our own disappointments and frustrations and crises, we discover what we're made of for better or worse. We learn that we too have a breaking point and are not as invincible as we like to think we are. If we're lucky, we might even get a fresh dose of empathy.

We, the caregivers, supporters, hand-holders, hug-givers, and friends of those experiencing loss, have a critical role to play.

Crisis teaches us that we are not in control, but will always have a choice. We all have something of value to offer our friends in their grief, even if it's just the choice to be brave. Sometimes, being brave is simply showing up with our broken hearts and feeling all the feelings. When people experience loss, their hearts are fragile and overwhelmed. Those of us who've walked our own journeys of triumph and tragedy understand the challenges, but we also know a secret: Nothing is ever wasted. It might not ever look the way we think it should or the way it still could be, if not for this or that. It won't be fair or forgotten. It won't be easily accepted or explained away. We'll long for a perfect world and wake up to a world that is far from it. Despite it all, we will wake up, though, some days, it may feel more like a curse than a blessing. Each passing day will bring with it a new mercy and, somehow, we rise up stronger, wiser, more attuned to the needs of others and more capable of assessing need. Through our pain, we are able to have a deeper understanding of those in emotional anguish and love them through their suffering.

We must make every effort to champion even the smallest of decisions because, without them, the big decisions are impossible.

I am truly in awe at the resiliency of the human spirit. I never tire of hearing about the incredible power that emerges from the ashes of brokenness. As Shauna Niequist noticed, "Most of the really significant and shaping moments of my life would [have been] unrecognizable to anyone but me."[5] For our friends wrestling through their loss and fighting for their healing, this will likely ring true as well. What may seem unimpressive to onlookers, might be a defining moment in the life of a person who is grieving. Perhaps the mere decision to keep fighting through the pain is their most personal and pivotal moment of all. We must make every effort to champion even the smallest of decisions because, without them, the big decisions are impossible. When the people we love are hurting, our job is to be there for them, meet them in the pain, and love them the best way we know how.

We love them when we drop the act and admit we struggle too.

We love them when we are emotionally available to them in their time of need.

We love them when we create a safe space for them to be honest.

We love them when we are kind and empathetic.

We love them when we are present and willing to listen.

We love them when we are patient and respect their healing process.

We love them when we refuse to diminish their experience or pretend we have all the answers.

We love them when we don't suggest a better way for them to grieve or try to toughen them up.

We love them when we offer them our strength and support when they are weary.

We love them when we give them permission to be weak.

We love them when we intercede on their behalf through prayer.

We love them when we understand healing is gradual but remind them they are making strides.

We love them when we see the depth of their pain, but also see beyond it.

As we continue to love our friends and walk with them on the journey to healing and wholeness, this is my prayer for all of us:

"Make us glad for as many days as you have afflicted us, for as many years as we have seen trouble. May your deeds be shown to your servants, your splendor to their children. May the favor [beauty] of the Lord our God rest on us; establish the work of our hands for us—yes, establish the work of our hands."[6]

EPILOGUE

During times of personal grief and uncertainty about my future, I have drawn immense comfort and encouragement from music. Since I also love words, I pay attention to the lyrics as well as the melodies, and I am often in awe of the richness I find hidden inside many old hymns.

As a musician, I feel privileged to sing over the brokenhearted, knowing that my words have the power to help them heal, and to remind the suffering that they are not alone in their pain. It is my hope that my songs impact will someone else's life the way so many other musicians have impacted mine.

The ideas I have written about on these pages, started as a song and eventually grew into a book. As I wrote each lyric, I realized there was so much more to unpack and explore, so I kept writing. The result is two-fold, as I have now written a song and book—both a labor of love. Each chapter title is a line of a lyric; each lyric, a hint of a deeper conversation.

For those of you who have journeyed with me thus far, thank you. The following pages contain the lyrics to a few original songs I have written and two hymns that have sustained me in my darkest moments. I wrote them (or included them) with you in mind and pray they comfort you when you need it most.

ABOUT THE AUTHOR

Brittany Barbera is musician, author, and artist from Bethlehem, Pennsylvania, who has found a second home in Nashville, Tennessee, where she currently resides. This singer/songwriter and first-time author has big things to say and the lyrics and lungs to back it up. Through her music and her writing, Barbera articulates the things so many people struggle to explain, even to themselves. Her wisdom, empathy, and humor spill over into her art, and find their way into the hearts of her loving fans.

Inspired by artists who have an affinity for exploring the texture of their voices, the rich nuance in Barbera's vocals leave listeners holding on to those notes a little longer each time. In 2013, she released her debut album, titled "The Sparrow," featuring songs such as "When the Well Runs Dry," and "Greater than my Faith." The album is available for purchase on iTunes.

Barbera is anxiously awaiting the release of her new single, "Let Me Be Weak," a companion to this book, and plans to record her next album in early 2016. When she is not singing or writing, you will likely find her making a mess in the pottery studio, taking a walk, searching for a new adventure, or trying to talk someone into becoming her personal chef.

LET ME BE WEAK

Words and Music by Brittany Barbera

I know I seem alright,
But it's been a long and lonely fight
I can see I need a safe place to land
Would you be kind and hold out your hand?

You don't have to find the words to say
'Cause we don't always know if we're gonna be okay
So don't try to fix me
I don't need your critique
Just be strong
Let me be weak

When there's nothing left to do,
You'll have to pray me through
Give me time; I need to heal
I don't want to hide the way I feel

YET I WILL PRAISE

Words by Brittany Barbera
Music by Brittany Barbera and Ben Neumann

My world is crashing down, yet I will praise
And nothing in me feels okay, yet I will praise
Amid the wreckage of my life—the hard days, even harder
nights
Yet I will praise
I will praise

You never leave, you won't forsake the one you love
But I question if your grace will be enough
Spill your mercy 'til my thirsty soul erupts
And I can say,
Yet I will praise
I will praise

Hope is distant, trials fierce, as days turn into many years
Yet I will praise, I will praise
And there's no fruit upon the vine, and I can't see a reason
why
Yet I will praise, I will praise

BE STILL MY SOUL

Words by Catharina von Schlegel, Translated by Jane Borthwick, Composer: Jean Sibelius

Be still, my soul; the Lord is on thy side;
Bear patiently the cross of grief or pain;
Leave to thy God to order and provide;
In every change He faithful will remain.
Be still, my soul; thy best, thy heavenly, Friend
Through thorny ways leads to a joyful end.

Be still, my soul; thy God doth undertake
To guide the future as He has the past.
Thy hope, thy confidence, let nothing shake;
All now mysterious shall be bright at last.
Be still, my soul; the waves and winds still know
His voice who ruled them while He dwelt below.

Be still, my soul, though dearest friends depart
And all is darkened in the vale of tears;
Then shalt thou better know His love, His heart,
Who comes to soothe thy sorrows and thy fears.
Be still, my soul; thy Jesus can repay
From His own fullness all He takes away.

Be still, my soul; the hour is hastening on
When we shall be forever with the Lord,
When disappointment, grief, and fear are gone,
Sorrow forgot, love's purest joys restored.
Be still, my soul; when change and tears are past,
All safe and blessed we shall meet at last.

GOD MOVES IN A MYSTERIOUS WAY

Words by William Cowper

God moves in a mysterious way
His wonders to perform;
He plants His footsteps in the sea
And rides upon the storm.

Deep in unfathomable mines
Of never failing skill
He treasures up His bright designs
And works His sov'reign will.

Ye fearful saints, fresh courage take;
The clouds ye so much dread
Are big with mercy and shall break
In blessings on your head.

Judge not the Lord by feeble sense,
But trust Him for His grace;
Behind a frowning providence
He hides a smiling face.

His purposes will ripen fast,
Unfolding every hour;
The bud may have a bitter taste,
But sweet will be the flow'r.

Blind unbelief is sure to err
And scan His work in vain;
God is His own interpreter,
And He will make it plain.

NOTES

Introduction

1. *"Stories are thought to be a particularly effective means of transmitting culture"*: Peggy Yuhas Buyers, *Organizational Communication: Theory and Behavior* (Boston, MA: Allyn and Bacon, 1997) 205.
2. *"Empathy"*: Tom Rath, *StrengthsFinder 2.0* (New York, NY: Gallup Press, 2007), 97-100. My friend Jordan introduced me to this book a few years ago and I immediately went out and bought a copy. I'm obsessed with personality profiles and it's not uncommon for me to force my friends to take them repeatedly. You should buy this book and then do the same. I'm sure your friends will be happy you did, and they won't be annoyed at all.
3. *"Empathy is the ability to project oneself into someone else's narrative"*: Jamie George, "Remember." Sermon, Journey Church, Franklin, TN, September 11, 2011. Jamie is a pastor, author, and speaker. For additional information, please visit www.jamiegeorge.com.

Chapter 1: "I Know I Seem Alright"

1. *"External bravado is often a cover-up for internal fear"*: Scott Sauls, "When You Feel Damaged, Invisible, and Irrelevant," Scott Sauls: God, People, Places, and Things (blog), August 8, 2015, http://scottsauls.com/2015/08/19/when-you-feel-messed-up-damaged-invisible-and-irrelevant (accessed November 7, 2015).
2. *"[We] can only love and be loved"*: John Ortberg, "John

Ortberg Quotes," Brainy Quotes (website), http://www.brainyquote.com/quotes/quotes/j/johnort ber526286.html (accessed November 29, 2015).

3. *"Goffman introduces us to the concept of 'impression management'"*: Erving Goffman, *Presentation of Self in Everyday Life* (Garden City, NJ: Doubleday, 1959), 16-17. Goffman has always fascinated me. He spent much of his career studying the mundane—all the little things we are not even likely to notice. But, as it turns out, most of life is lived out in these seemingly insignificant interactions. While his books are a little challenging to read because they are so intellectual, I'd still recommend them.

4. *"He identifies two distinct kinds of activity present in each interaction"*: Erving Goffman, *Presentation of Self in Everyday Life* (Garden City, NJ: Doubleday, 1959), 1-17.

5. *"Don't compare what [we] know about [ourselves]"*: Darren Whitehead, "Message," Sermon, For the City: A Study in the Book of Acts, Church of the City, Nashville, TN, October 20, 2013. To listen to the sermon in its entirety, please visit http://churchofthecity.com.

Chapter 2: "But It's Been a Long and Lonely Fight"

1. *"When [people] feel you are challenging [them]"*: Matt Abrahams, "Think Fast, Talk Smart: Communication Techniques," Lecture, Stanford University Graduate School of Business, Stanford, CA, October 25, 2014. To watch to the full presentation, please visit https://youtu.be/HAnw168huqA (accessed November 7, 2015).

2. *"Loneliness creates a deep psychological wound"*: Guy Winch, "How to Practice Emotional Hygiene," Lecture, TED

Talk, Växjö, Sweden, November 2014. To watch the talk, please visit https://youtu.be/F2hc2FLOdhI (accessed November 7, 2015). Guy Winch is a psychologist, speaker, and author of two books, including *Emotional First Aid: Healing Rejection, Guilt, Failure and Other Everyday Hurts* (http://www.amazon.com/Emotional-First-Aid-Rejection-Everyday/dp/0142181072).

3. *"Eisenberger discovered that the feeling of being excluded"*: Naomi Eisenberger, M. Lieberman, and K. Williams, "Does Rejection Hurt? An FMRO Study of Social Exclusion." U.S. National Library of Medicine (October 10, 2003). To view the research findings, refer to http://www.ncbi.nlm.nih.gov/pubmed/14551436 (accessed August 12, 2015).

4. *"I have surely seen the affliction of my people who are in Egypt and have heart their cry"*: Exodus 3:7-8a.

5. *"His 'eye affects [His] heart'"*: Adam Clarke, "Commentary on the Bible: Exodus Chapter 3 [1861]." Internet Sacred Text Archive. http://www.sacred-texts.com/bib/cmt/clarke/exo003.htm (accessed November 28, 2015).

Chapter 3: "I Need a Safe Place to Land"

1. *"If we could read the secret history of our enemies"*: Henry Wadsworth Longfellow, *The Literary News (New Series) Volume 3* (New York, NY: F. Leypoldt, 1883), 122.

2. *"When you are in the middle of a story it isn't a story at all"*: Margaret Atwood, *Alias Grace: A Novel* (New York, NY: Anchor Books, 1997), 298.

3. *"When it comes to vulnerability, connectivity means sharing our stories with people who've earned the right to hear them"*: Brené Brown, *Daring Greatly: How the Courage to Be Vulnerable Transforms the Way We Live, Love, Parent, and Lead* (New

York, NY: Gotham Books, 2012). I cannot overstate my love for Brené Brown. If you have the opportunity to read her books or listen to her speak, take it. Her insights are brilliant and she backs up her work with scientific research, all the while writing in an accessible way. I'm still trying to figure out how to make her become my best friend, so let me know if you have any ideas.

4. *"The expectations of others can exert a subtle but controlling pressure"*: Brennan Manning, *Ragamuffin Gospel: Good News for the Bedraggled, Beat-up, and Burnt Out* (Sisters: Multnomah Books, 1990), 17. This is one of the best books I have ever read. Manning's words are simultaneously convicting and reassuring—a true reflection of the gospel message. It took me almost a year to finish this book, because after every couple of pages, I'd have to stop and reflect on what I read before I could read any further.

Chapter 4: "Would You Be Kind and Hold Out Your Hand?"

1. *"Everyone who moves toward the scene to help"*: Frank Ochberg, "When Helping Hurts: Sustaining Trauma Workers," Gift from Within: PTSD Resources for Survivors and Caregivers (website), 1998, http://www.giftfromwithin.org/pdf/helping.pdf (accessed September 16, 2015).

Chapter 5: "You Don't Have to Find the Words to Say"

1. *"Just because a person studies math"*: Lynn Cockett, Personal Communication, Juniata College, 2006. Lynn was my

favorite professor in college and she introduced me to some of the researchers I write about in this book, such as Goffman and Yuhas Buyers. I hope to scare her with my freakish ability to recall a conversation we had about a decade ago and ended up including in this chapter.

2. *"93% of all communication is nonverbal"*: Albert Mehrabian, Susan Ferris. *Journal of Consulting Psychology* 31 (1967): 248-252.

3. *"Our presence in a place of need is more powerful than 1,000 sermons"*: Chuck Colson. For additional information, please visit: http://chuckcolson.org.

4. *"Take the temperature of the room"*: Adrianne Haslet-Davis, Lecture, "What People Say When They Don't Know What to Say," TEDx Talk Beacon Street, Lincoln School, Brookline, MA, November 2014. To watch the full talk, please visit https://youtu.be/QuaIMgzIOn8 (accessed September 12, 2015) and to learn more about Haslet-Davis' latest endeavors, please refer to her personal website: http://www.adrianne-haslet-davis.com.

5. *"To me, all harmony is active listening"*: Joy Williams, Twitter, April 6 2011.

6. *"Harmony is defined, among other things, as 'agreement'"*: "Harmony," Dictionary.com, http://dictionary.reference.com/browse/harmony (accessed September 12, 2015).

7. *"People will forget what you said, people will forget what you did"*: Maya Angelou via Barbara Quirk, *Women Need to Feel Good About Themselves. The Capital Times,* July 22, 2003.

Chapter 6: "We Don't Always Know if We're Going to Be Okay"

1. *"A loud and cheerful greeting early in the morning will be taken as a curse"*: Proverbs 27:14 NLT. If you've been

struggling to find a "life verse," I think this one has real potential.

2. *"The difference between [us] and God is that God doesn't think He's [us]"*: Anne Lamott, "Quotable Quotes," Goodreads (website), https://www.goodreads.com/quotes/226355-the-difference-between-you-and-god-is-that-god-doesn-t (accessed Novem-ber 20, 2015).

3. *"We live by promises, not explanations"*: Larry Burd, Calvary Baptist Church, Bethlehem, PA, June 2010.

4. *"Then they came to Elim, where there were twelve springs of water and seventy palm trees"*: Exodus 15:27.

5. *"It signified to Israel once again"*: Crossway Bibles. "Exodus 15:27." ESV: study Bible: English standard version (Wheaton, Ill: Crossway Bibles, 2007), 170.

6. *"Grace will remake but not undo"*: Rowan Williams. Edited by Matheson Russell. *On Rowan Williams: Critical Essays (Eugene: Cascade Books, 2009), 125.*

7. *"Weep with those who weep"*: Romans 12:15.

8. *"And they shall call his name Immanuel, (which means, God with us)"*: Matthew 1:23.

9. *"To offer your beloved people Average and Boring is such grace"*: Anne Lamott, Twitter, January 9, 2015.

Chapter 7: "Don't Try to Fix Me; I Don't Need Your Critique"

1. *"It's not [their] fault"*: Goodwill Hunting. Directed by Gus Van Sant. Boston, MA: Miramax, 1997.

2. *"The problem is not our feelings"*: Jon Acuff, Lecture, "5 Club" at Cross Point Church, Franklin, TN, May 29, 2014.

3. *"One who loves a pure heart and who speaks with grace"*: Proverbs 22:11 NIV.

Chapter 8: "Just Be Strong"

1. *"Fear kills your potential"*: Apolo Anton Ohno, *Zero Regrets: Be Greater Than Yesterday* (New York, NY: Simon & Schuster, 2010), 194.
2. *"Even youths grow tired and weary"*: Isaiah 40:30-31 NIV.
3. *"Strength, inner strength, comes from receiving love"*: Donald Miller, *Blue Like Jazz: Non-religious thoughts on Christian Spirituality* (Nashville, TN: Thomas Nelson, 2003), 232.
4. *"But Moses' hands grew weary, so they took a stone and put it under him"*: Exodus 17:12.

Chapter 9: "Let Me Be Weak"

1. *"Just because you feel afraid as you confront a person or issue"*: Elizabeth Roethke, Personal Communication, Bethlehem, PA, 2011.
2. *"When you cannot ask for and accept help without [self] judgment"*: Brené Brown, Twitter and Oprah's Lifeclass, September 22, 2013. (accessed September 22, 2013).
3. *"Vulnerability is the last thing I want you to see in me, but the first thing I look for in you"*: Brené Brown, *Daring Greatly: How the Courage to Be Vulnerable Transforms the Way We Live, Love, Parent, and Lead* (New York, NY: Gotham Books, 2012), 113.
4. *"Get by with a little help from [our] friends"*: John Lennon, Paul McCartney, *"With A Little Help From My Friends"*, St. Pepper's Lonely Hearts Club Band, (London, England: EMI, 1967). I have to be honest here: If you're not thinking of the Joe Cocker version of this song right now, I'm not sure we can be friends.
5. *"I discovered an astonishing truth: God is attracted to weakness"*: Jim Cymbala, Dean Merrill, *Fresh Wind, Fresh Fire: What Happens When God's Spirit invades the Hearts of His People*

(Grand Rapids, MI: Zondervan, 1997), 19.

6. *"Honesty goes both ways. It acknowledges both weakness and strength"*: Dave Ohlerking, Ben Rogers, "Dave Ohlerking's Nuggets of Wisdom," Ben Rogers: The Journey Continues (blog), October 20, 2010, http://benrodgers.blogspot.com/2010/10/dave-ohlerkings-nuggets-of-wisdom.html (accessed November 7, 2015).

7. *"I was given a thorn in my flesh"*: 2 Corinthians 12:7 NIV.

8. *"Therefore I will boast all the more gladly about my weakness"*: 2 Corinthians 12:9 NIV.

9. *"In the kingdom of God, compassion is the currency of authority"*: Alan Scott, Lecture, New Wine Leaders Conference, United Kingdom, March 17-19, 2014.

10. *"He drew me up from the pit of destruction"*: Psalm 40:2.

11. *"And there I will give her vineyards and make the Valley of Achor [trouble] a door of hope"*: Hosea 2:15.

12. *"His father saw him and felt compassion, and ran and embraced him and kissed him"*: Luke 15:20.

13. *"The people dwelling in darkness have seen a great light"*: Matthew 4:16.

14. *"While they were talking and discussing together, Jesus himself drew near and went with them"*: Luke 24:15-16.

15. *"He chose the JV Team"*: J.R. Briggs. J.R. was my pastor for a short, but formative season. His teaching have stuck with me and helped me gain new insight on many Biblical stories and have given me a greater understanding of what it means to be "Jesus-ish." For further information, please visit http://www.jrbriggs.com.

16. *"His pleasure is not in the strength of the horse, nor his delight in the legs of the warrior"*: Psalm 147:10-11 NIV.

Chapter 10: "When There's Nothing Left to Do, You'll Have to Pray Me Through"

1. *"He delights in every detail of their lives"*: Psalm 37:23 NLT.
2. *"And he will be the stability of your times"*: Isaiah 33:6.
3. *"What is important is not the number of people praying"*: Timothy Keller, Twitter, April 19, 2013. I've enjoyed reading Keller's insights for many years. If you would like to listen to his sermons or read his books, please visit http://www.timothykeller.com.
4. *"History belongs to the intercessors"*: Walter Wink, *The Powers That Be: Theology for a New Millennium.* (New York, NY: Doubleday, 1999), 185-86.

Chapter 11: "Give Me Time; I Need to Heal"

1. *"Isn't it funny how day by day nothing changes"*: C.S. Lewis, "Quotable Quote," Goodreads (website), https://www.good-reads.com/quotes/583967-isn-t-it-funny-how-day-by-day-nothing-changes-but (accessed November 29, 2015).
2. *"Trust the winter seasons [of life]"*: "Nonurgency," Idle and Blessed (blog), July 22, 2015, http://jordan-idleandblessed.blogspot.com/2015/07/nonurgency.html (accessed August 1, 2015).

Chapter 12: "I Don't Want to Hide the Way I Feel"

1. *"Malcom Gladwell tells a story about a Nazi attack on London"*: Malcom Gladwell, David and Goliath (New York, NY: Little, Brown and Company, 2013).
2. *"We are all of us not merely liable to fear"*: J. T. MacCurdy, *The Structure of Morale* (New York, NY: Cambridge

University Press, 1943), 1-26.

3. *"The public had three distinct responses"*: J. T. MacCurdy, *The Structure of Morale* (New York, NY: Cambridge University Press, 1943), 13-14.

4. *"The beginning of love is to let those we love be perfectly themselves"*: Thomas Merton, *No Man Is an Island* (Boston, MA: Shambhala Publications, 2005), 177-178.

5. *"Most of the really significant and shaping moments of my life would be unrecognizable"*: Shauna Niequist, "Why You Should Stop Waiting for Life to Be Perfect," Storyline (blog), June 9, 2015, http://storylineblog.com/2015/06/09/why-you-should-stop-waiting-for-life-to-be-perfect (accessed September 25, 2015).

6. *"Make us glad for as many years as you have afflicted us"*: Psalm 90:15-17 NIV.

Epilogue

1. *"Be still my soul, the Lord is on thy side"*: Catharina von Schlegel (1752), Translated by Jane Borthwick (1855), "Be Still My Soul," Lutheran Hymnals. http://www.lutheran-hymnal.com/lyrics/tlh651.htm (accessed September 26, 2015).

2. *"God moves in a mysterious way, his wonders to perform"*: William Cowper (1774), "God Moves in a Mysterious Way," Timeless Truths: Free Online Library. http://library.timelesstruths.org/music/God_Moves_in_a_Mysterious_Way (accessed Septem-ber 26, 2015).

"LET ME BE WEAK"

SELF-PUBLISHING
SCHOOL

NOW IT'S YOUR TURN

Discover the EXACT 3-step blueprint you need to become a bestselling author in 3 months.

Self-Publishing School helped me, and now I want them to help you with this FREE VIDEO SERIES!

Even if you're busy, bad at writing, or don't know where to start, you CAN write a bestseller and build your best life.

With tools and experience across a variety niches and professions, Self-Publishing School is the only resource you need to take your book to the finish line!

DON'T WAIT

Watch this FREE VIDEO SERIES now, and Say "YES" to becoming a bestseller:

WATCH THE VIDEO SERIES:
(https://xe172.isrefer.com/go/firstbook/brittanybarbera)

THANK YOU FOR PURCHASING MY BOOK!

I really appreciate your feedback,
and I love hearing what you have to say.

Please leave me a helpful review on Amazon letting me
know what you thought of the book.

Connect with me:

Web: BrittanyBarbera.com
Facebook: Brittany Barbera
Twitter: @BrittanyBarbera

Thanks so much!

- Brittany Barbera

www.ingramcontent.com/pod-product-compliance
Lightning Source LLC
LaVergne TN
LVHW041319080426
835513LV00008B/519